Going Sideways

Other Books by Duane Pederson

Jesus People
On Lonely Street with God
Day of Miracles (co-author with Helen Kooiman)

Other Books by Helen Kooiman

Joyfully Expectant: Meditations Before Baby Comes
Please Pray for the Cabbages: Pint-Size Parables for Grown-ups
Small Talk
Living Words of Comfort and Cheer
Cameos: Women Fashioned by God
Transformed: Behind the Scenes with Billy Graham
Silhouettes: Women Behind Great Men
Walter Knott: Keeper of The Flame
Forgiveness in Action
Day of Miracles (co-author with Duane Pederson)

Going Sideways

HOPE,
LOVE, LIFE
VERSUS
SUICIDE

DUANE PEDERSON
and HELEN W. KOOIMAN

HAWTHORN BOOKS, INC.
W. Clement Stone, Publisher
NEW YORK

ACKNOWLEDGMENTS

Much research and study preceded the writing of this book. In particular, the authors are indebted to the following for help and inspiration received: *Suicide,* Earl A. Grollman, Beacon Press, Boston, Copyright © 1971 by Earl A. Grollman; *The Bell Jar,* Sylvia Plath, Harper & Row, N.Y., Copyright © 1971 by Harper & Row; *The Savage God,* A. Alvarez, Random House, N.Y., Copyright © 1970, 1971, 1972 by A. Alvarez; *Theory of Suicide,* Maurice L. Farber, Funk & Wagnalls, N.Y., Copyright © 1968 by Maurice L. Farber; *Suicide: The Gamble with Death,* Gene Lester and David Lester, Prentice-Hall, Englewood Cliffs, N.J., Copyright © 1971 by Prentice-Hall; *Suicidal Behavior,* J. Wallace McCulloch and Alistair E. Philip, Pergamon Press, N.Y., Copyright © 1972 by J. W. McCulloch and A. E. Philip; *Social Forces in Urban Suicide,* Ronald W. Maris, The Dorsey Press, Homewood, Ill., Copyright © The Dorsey Press 1969. *Suicide* (pamphlet), Henri Blocher translated by Roger Van Dyk, Inter-Varsity Press, Downers Grove, Ill., Copyright © 1972 by InterVarsity; *The Lengthening Shadow of Suicide* (pamphlet), Russell Palmer, Claretian Publications, Chicago, Ill., Copyright © 1965 by Claretian Publications; "Go to the Top for Help," Anonymous, *These Times* magazine, November, 1972; "Up from Suicide" (editorial), *Christianity Today* magazine, June 9, 1972; *The Living Bible,* Kenneth Taylor, Tyndale House Publishers, Wheaton, Ill., Copyright © 1971 by Tyndale House; *Understanding and Counseling the Suicidal Person,* Paul W. Pretzel, Abingdon, Nashville, Tenn., Copyright © 1972 by Abingdon.

Library of Congress Catalog Card Number: 74-335
ISBN: 0-8015-3056-3

1 2 3 4 5 6 7 8 9 10

Contents

1824214

Preface

Suicide! The whispered word. The taboo subject. "Going sideways," young people call it today. By any name it is ugly and unnecessary—an insult to humanity, an affront to God, the community, and society.

Suicide is a problem growing in intensity, and no one is immune. Suicide appears in all ages, in both sexes, and on every economic level, with no geographic boundaries.

The seriousness of the suicide problem has hit both of us as we have read letters relating suicide attempts or accounts of completed suicides and as we have faced the magnitude of the problem of depression and its devastating consequences in our own lives. Allowed to go unchecked, depression can so engulf us that we actually hand ourselves over to our enemy, the devil. We can become "swallowed up with overmuch sorrow," as the Apostle Paul describes it.

The Bible speaks of men who wished to die. God didn't answer their death wish but, instead, chose to lift them up and used them mightily. Tragically, the Bible also records some suicides. Tragic is the right word! These men had recourse to forgiveness, to sustaining power, and to the grace, mercy, and love of God. Each of them could have lived complete and fulfilled lives. How tragic that they didn't. How tragic when anyone doesn't!

And so this book has been written—not because we particularly enjoyed examining this depressing and touchy subject but out of a sense of need, a sense of addressing ourselves to what we see as a growing problem that can even affect Christians.

This book offers understanding and sympathy to those so

overwhelmed by the vicissitudes of life that they have sought escape through suicide but have failed in their attempt. It also examines motives and lays bare some facts that are often over-looked. We do this in a spirit of love and genuine concern.

Loving acceptance and open communication can move a person out of suicidal preoccupation when he is shown that there is hope and a reason for living. This we have tried to do. The psalmist asked, "Why art thou cast down, O my soul?" And we ask it, too. "Why art thou disquieted in me? Why downcast? Why be discouraged and sad? Why be depressed and gloomy? Trust in God! Praise Him for His wondrous help; He will make you smile again" (our paraphrase of Pss. 42:5; 43:5). Yes, we *strongly* recommend this: "Hope thou in God" (Ps. 42:5, *AV*).

Going Sideways

1

Could Something Be Missing?

Life is a battle in which we fall from the wounds we receive in running away.
John Rannell

"Please kill me, Lord; I'd rather be dead than alive." Then the Lord said, "Is it right to be angry about this?"
*Jonah's complaint and God's reply,
Jonah 4:1–4, AV**

"Within the last year three of my friends tried to commit suicide. Life was too much for them. They couldn't hack it. This world ate them up until their only thought of escape was death. Could something be missing?"

So began a letter to the *Hollywood Free Paper*—only one of hundreds relating the same sad story of attempted suicide or completed suicide. Could something be missing? That is a good question, the right question. People have been killing themselves since the beginning of recorded history, and it is safe to say that

---

* Biblical quotations bearing the notation *AV* come from *The Authorized (King James) Version*. All other biblical quotations are taken from *The Living Bible*.

3

in every instance something is missing. There are many motives for suicide. This book will attempt to examine some of them. Suicide is a complex problem and is becoming more so in our increasingly complex society.

Consider these cries: "Lord, take away my life"; or "O Lord, take my life from me, for it is better for me to die than to live"; or "I am not able to bear all this. . . . It is too heavy for me. . . . Kill me, I pray thee." Sound familiar? Perhaps you've anguished in prayer like that or someone you know has cried out like this. They may even have ended up a suicide statistic.

Are you aware that those cries were uttered by some very well-known Bible characters? Moses the meek, remember him? He had achieved stupendous things for God and his nation, but he carried some unbelievable burdens on his shoulders. It was he who, physically exhausted, overtaxed by the unremitting daily strain of maintaining liaison between God and a nation of two million discontented people, having reached and passed the limit of endurance, and overwhelmed with a sense of complete and utter failure, cried out in anguish,

> Why pick on me, to give me the burden of a people like this? Are they my children? Am I their father? Is that why you have given me the job of nursing them along like babies until we get to the land you promised their ancestors? Where am I supposed to get meat for all these people? For they weep to me saying, "Give us meat!" I can't carry this nation by myself! The load is far too heavy! If you are going to treat me like this, please kill me right now; it will be a kindness. Let me out of this impossible situation (Num. 11:11–15).

What Moses couldn't possibly know was that many, many years of wonderful service for God still lay ahead of him. Did God answer his prayer? No way!

It is a very serious thing when a believer—one who has placed his life in God's hands, trusting Christ as his Savior—is robbed of his desire to live. Yes, even for such as these something is missing.

Look at a lone figure sitting forlornly under a broom bush out in the wilderness. He had traveled all day, fleeing for his life. Hot in pursuit, anxious to kill him, were the men sent by Queen Jezebel. Elijah had killed the wicked prophets of Baal—no small task, for 1 Kings 18:22 tells us that Baal had 450 prophets! The Lord gave special strength to Elijah (1 Kings 18:46), but now, fresh from the most dramatic scene one can possibly imagine, where he had been the divine instrument in the hands of God, Elijah wilts. He sprawls exhausted, emotionally and physically, totally unfit to meet the threats of the raging Jezebel. Listen to him as he prays that he might die: "I've had enough," he tells the Lord. "Take away my life. I've got to die sometime, and it might as well be now" (1 Kings 19:4).

Although Elijah felt that he had been driven to banishment and obscurity—things were much too hot for him in the land of Israel—and although he wished to die, God was still not through with him. God deals with us in so much better a way than we actually deserve. What if God were actually to take us at our word and grant us our foolish passionate requests? We may lose ourselves, as it were, like Elijah in a wilderness, but we are not lost to the watchful loving care and eye of the Lord when we are His children. For want of foresight we don't know how to pray often as we ought, but God's grace is sufficient. His provision is enough to meet our every need. He *will* take care of us. He took care of Elijah, keeping him alive, feeding him by ravens, then by an angel, and then while he traveled in a maze through the desert for forty days without meat or food. God sustained and encouraged Elijah and in due time brought him out alive.

Have you ever said, "I'd rather be dead than alive"? You were only echoing what Jonah, the prophet who ran away from God, said at one time. God had given a difficult assignment to Jonah, but Jonah forgot that God is with us in these difficult places, and he took off in the opposite direction. Instead of going to Nineveh, he went down to the seacoast port of Joppa, where he found a ship leaving for Tarshish. He ended up inside the belly of a great fish after he had been thrown overboard into the raging sea by the ship's crew.

The interior of a great sea monster is a strange place to have a prayer meeting, but Jonah had a confrontation with God in the ocean's depths. Jonah said something very profound (which he later forgot). He said, "When I had lost all hope, I turned my thoughts once more to the Lord" (Jon. 2:7). Surely when we are plunged to the very pit of despair, we, like Jonah, must remember to turn our thoughts once more to the Lord. Can we not learn from Jonah's horrible experience that if we would not run away from God, if we would not take our thoughts off him to begin with, we wouldn't get into such trouble or feel "locked out of life," as Jonah put it?

The Lord ordered the fish to spit up Jonah on the beach, and it did. Then the Lord spoke to Jonah again: "Go to that great city, Nineveh," He said, "and warn them of their doom, as I told you to before!" (Jon. 2:10; 3:1–2).

This time Jonah obeyed and returned to deliver God's message to wicked Nineveh. To his amazement and dismay he saw that vast city turn to God; revival swept through it and its extensive suburbs. But then—and it is so difficult to understand why—Jonah got very angry. The Bible says that when God saw that the inhabitants of the city stopped their evil ways, He abandoned His plan to destroy them (Jon. 3:10).

Instead of leaping for joy, praising and thanking God, what did Jonah do? He went outside the city, sat sulking under a gourd, and complained:

This is exactly what I thought you'd do, Lord, when I was there in my own country and you first told me to come here.

That's why I ran away to Tarshish. For I knew you were a gracious God, merciful, slow to get angry, and full of kindness; I knew how easily you could cancel your plans for destroying these people. Please kill me, Lord; I'd rather be dead than alive (when nothing I told them happens).

Then the Lord said, "Is it right to be angry about this" (Jon. 4:1-4)?

But even while Jonah sat there moaning and feeling sorry for himself because his predictions hadn't come true and he felt like a fool, God was taking pity on him. When the leaves of the shelter he had erected to shade himself from the heat began to wither, the Lord arranged for a vine to grow up quickly and spread its broad leaves over Jonah's head to shade him. This made him comfortable and very grateful (Jon. 4:5).

For the second time Jonah expresses the death wish (Jon. 4:8). The first time Jonah felt God had shattered his reputation as a prophet. He had prophesied judgment, and God had exercised mercy. Since his reputation was gone, Jonah concluded that it would be better to die than to live. There are those who believe that, the second time, Jonah might have experienced something physical, such as sunstroke, which might have left him sick enough to wish to die.

God had to reprimand Jonah again and said, "Is it right for you to be angry because the plant died?"

"Yes," Jonah said, "it is; it is right for me to be angry enough to die!"

Then the Lord said, "You feel sorry for yourself when your shelter is destroyed, though you did no work to put it there, and it is, at best, short-lived. And why shouldn't I feel sorry for a great city like Nineveh with its 120,000 people in utter spiritual darkness" (Jon. 4:7-10).

Moses, Elijah, and Jonah—three men, all mightily used by God, yet so much like us in our frailty and human weakness—so prone to complaining, feeling sorry for ourselves, indulging in self-pity, resentful even of God's grace and mercy.

Did it come as a surprise to you to learn that these men of God should have wished to die? Did you feel that such as these should be beyond and above feelings of discouragement and depression? Could something have been missing in their lives, too? What brings on thoughts of suicide and the expression of the death wish?

Thank God He has left us the biblical record. It's all there to help and instruct us, and to encourage us, too. The biographies of God's heroes are written for our needs today. The Bible is very contemporary. These men were God's heroes, but they were very human. We don't have to apologize for our humanness. As the well-known Gert Behanna, former alcoholic, whose story is told in *The Late Liz,* once said, "God must have thought an awful lot of us humans; after all, he came in the flesh!"

Just because they copped out on God along the line for a brief period of time, God didn't cop out on them. But how much better it is to learn the lessons from such as these so that we don't have to go through what they did. We don't have to long for death or contemplate suicide. There is a better way to cope with life's complexities. Could something be missing from your life?

2

Suicide: The Swallowing Up

Suicide is Satan's gateway to defeat, but
Christ is the "Door" to freedom and victory!

Anonymous

It would be simplistic, unwise, unfair, and unrealistic to say that
the thing that is missing in the lives of all those who commit
suicide is a relationship with God through Jesus Christ. Such a
blanket generalization is far too often thrown over what many
consider "the scandal of suicide." A generalization like that is
most unkind to the memory of the person who took his own
life, only adds to the hurt and heartache of the victim's family,
and causes his friends needless distress. It relegates the suicide
to hell, banished forever from the presence of God and loved
ones who may have preceded him in death and others who will
surely ultimately follow him in death.

Of course, it is distressing and disappointing when one who

has professed faith in Christ takes his life with deliberate intent. Someone wrote to the Billy Graham "My Answer" newspaper column and asked whether a Christian who committed suicide could be saved? The writer stated that a wonderful Christian in her church had committed suicide and that it was a shock to everyone. The suicide victim was known to be a sweet, considerate person. It threw everyone in the church and raised many questions.

The answer is that only the Lord knows the circumstances surrounding the person's death. Billy Graham replied,

> You say this person was "the sweetest, most considerate Christian" you ever met. Without judging, it is possible that she was all you say she was, and yet without a personal relationship to Christ. There are many kind, winsome people who are not believers.
>
> The other possibility is: if she were really a Christian and took her own life, she certainly must have been mentally deranged. Christians are not immune to mental sickness, and self-destruction is often a symptom of insanity. When this happens, it is distressing and disappointing, for we think of the Christian faith as the very thing which helps us to rise above our weaknesses and deficiencies, and it does, all things being equal. But when a Christian, due to mental derangement, takes his life, we must believe that God who is merciful will not hold such a one responsible.

At one time it was thought that everyone who committed suicide was mentally deranged, but that has been disproved. What is known, however, is that the suicide is always a desperate person, one who has lost all hope. Thus, it can be safely said that the thing that is missing in the life of a suicide is hope. He may not be totally mentally deranged, but at the very moment he commits the act of killing himself he is acting out of sheer desperation. Life has lost its meaning; the situation in which he finds himself appears hopeless. Death becomes an emergency exit that frees him from facing the immediate present and the inevitable tomorrow with its pain and problems.

We find Ben Haden's outlook on suicide a refreshing change from those who would sit so harshly in judgment upon the suicide victim. Mr. Haden says, and we agree, "There's nothing that turns my stomach more than to see Christians who sit down and speculate on where someone driven to the point of suicide will spend eternity. That's up to *God* . . . it's *not* up to you or me." [1]

The fact cannot be ignored, however, that there are those who do commit suicide who have not had a vital personal encounter with the living Christ. What is missing in their lives is a definite relationship to God through Christ. These people believe suicide will "end it all" but fail to realize that suicide is *not* actually the ultimate in the "geographic cure." It only changes their location from earth to hell. This is an undeniable reality confirmed by the Bible.

One minister warned a would-be suicide that if he persisted in trying to take his own life, the place to which he would go was far worse than was the situation he presently found himself in here on earth. "You had better stay around and find God's solution for your dilemma!" he was kindly admonished. "Ending it all is no solution. Jesus Christ is. Let Him live His life in you. It was the Apostle Paul who said, 'Christ lives in me. And the real life I now have within this body is a result of my trusting in the Son of God, who loves me and gave himself for me' " (Gal. 2:20).

The Bible assures us that when we are willing to face our difficulties, committing our lives to God and then trusting Him to work out His perfect will in our lives, then we can be more than conquerers through Him who loved us. If there is one thing the Bible does make clear, it is the fact that we can expect trouble and problems in this life. No one is exempted from some

degree of situational problems, painful illness, distressing loneliness, disabling handicaps, money problems, stormy love affairs,
difficult interpersonal relationships, domestic difficulties, old age,
or anxiety in one form or another.

We all need a large "cope-scope"! Acknowledging our own
weakness and inability to cope is not a sign of weakness. In fact,
it is a good thing to turn to God and say, "Look, this is more
than I can take. I simply don't understand everything that's
happening to me and the situation in the world around me.
It all appears utterly futile and hopeless. What's the use? If You've
got any solutions and can help me cope, then, Lord, I'm more
than willing to exchange my weakness for Your strength." The
Apostle Paul could say in his time of trauma and weakness, "I
can do all things through Christ which strengtheneth me"
(Phil. 4:13, *AV*).

Hardship and suffering were not foreign to Paul. Prior to
making the above statement he had said, "I have learned how to
get along happily whether I have much or little. I know how to
live on almost nothing or with everything. I have learned the
secret of contentment in every situation, whether it be a full
stomach or hunger, plenty or want" (Phil. 4:11, 12). He knew
what it was to be in bonds and imprisoned. Deprivation, sickness,
persecution, loneliness—all of these and more were within his
experience. What was he saying? Only that whatever the circumstances, he could handle them, because he transferred the weight
of them all to God, trusting Him to work out His perfect will
in His life. It was Christ Who strengthened him. In the power of
His might, Paul said he could endure (Eph. 6:10).

To young Timothy, his son in the faith, he could wisely say
from practical experience that it is possible to be strengthened
with might by God's Spirit working in the inner man, which
strength comes from the grace that is in Christ Jesus (2 Tim. 2:1).
The manner in which he stated this indicated a present and

continued supply of strength that made him equal to whatever confronted him.

These were not just pretty, pious-sounding words conjured up by a man with a unique talent for expressing himself well. Here was a man who had been the most aggressive and influential enemy of the early Church. He was its bitterest persecutor. He had been on both sides of the fence—against Christ and then all-out for him. His was as complex a personality as one can meet within the pages of the Bible. He was both conservative and radical, venturesome and cautious. He possessed an excess of zeal, which was bent on destroying every vestige of Christianity until he had an amazing confrontation with Christ on the road to Damascus. Paul was the most difficult kind of man to convert; therefore, if you think you are an impossible breed, utterly beyond the reach of the help of God through Christ, then a long look at the Apostle Paul is in order for you.

If Paul's life could be salvaged, so can yours. It has been said that suicide is Satan's gateway to defeat, but Christ is the only "Door" to freedom and victory! Paul learned this as he faced the harassment of those who opposed Christ just as he himself had once done. Weariness and pain, hunger and thirst, cold and nakedness, beatings and imprisonments, stoning and shipwreck, perils on land and on sea, were his missionary experience (2 Cor. 11:23–28). How did he react? Did he wish to die? Did he seek the door of escape through suicide? He did not. He lived through all of this, not just passively enduring what was happening to him but actually glorying in his infirmities so that the power of Christ might rest upon him (2 Cor. 12:9). Paul could say, "I will suffer, I will bear reproach, I will be bold."

Paul was writing to those who were being persecuted for naming themselves Christians. His counsel to them was to people who were enduring great trouble, whose very lives were often in danger. So when he said, "Whatever happens, dear friends, be glad in the Lord" (Phil. 3:1), he was actually speaking to those whose situation looked anything but promising. Was there much to be glad about? Wasn't everything pretty hopeless? Yes, things were grim. Paul reminded them, "Put your trust and hope in Christ alone. . . . This is the only way to experience His mighty power on your behalf" (Phil. 3:7).

Did Paul ever express the death wish? Did the thought of dying enter into his thinking? It did, but not exactly in the way of one who contemplates suicide, it may be said with reasonable certainty. Paul expressed it like this: "I am in a strait betwixt two, having a desire to depart, and to be with Christ; which is far better; nevertheless to abide in the flesh is more needful for you" (Phil. 1:23–24, *AV*). Paul was saying that living means opportunities for Christ, and dying—well, that's better yet! But if living will give me more opportunities to win people to Christ, then I really don't know which is better, to live or die. Sometimes I want to live and at other times I don't, for I long to go and be with Christ. How much happier for me than being here! But the fact is that I can be of more help to you by staying. Yes, I am still needed down here and so I feel certain I will be staying on earth a little longer, to help you grow and become happy in your faith (Phil. 1:21–25).

Paul definitely looked forward to death as a release from life's vicissitudes, but as long as he was in the land of the living he would show himself to be a channel of God's grace and great love. The thing that Paul had going for him that many who take their own lives apparently do not possess in adequate measure was a total selflessness. His focus was on Christ and the giving of His life to secure salvation and the rewards and beauties of heaven for him and all those who would acknowledge and receive Him.

Paul was able to look away from his own discomforts, the threats on his life, the physical infirmity that he described as "a thorn in the flesh," and the uncertainties that surrounded his existence, and in so doing he could "keep on keeping on." He described life as a race in which a good runner exerts every bit of physical energy to win; life was a battle in which the good soldier puts on that which equips him to fight a good fight.

But always his dependency was upon Christ, and he urged his hearers to keep their eyes likewise on Jesus. My hope in Christ is steadfast, Paul could say, and my consolation comes from Him. This was no idle boast or trumped up spiritualizing. He was speaking from experience—life was tough, a real battle, a long difficult race with many obstacles thrown in the way. There were hurdles to overcome and the enemy to fight. To endure, a man had to have a strategy and inner fortification.

It was of immense help when one's brothers and sisters in Christ were for him, not working against him, Paul had discovered; and so he cautioned against all sorts of things that we can do unthinkingly or deliberately that impede our own or others' progress in the Christian life. We are to love each other and show it. We are patiently and kindly to help those who are going through difficult times. Forgive each other and comfort one another, Paul strongly advised. The reason? If a person is going through great anguish and grief, if the problems loom high, we are not to add to his affliction. Paul said that unless a person receives help from others that can instill some hope within him, he may be "swallowed up with overmuch sorrow" (2 Cor. 2:7, *AV*).

Unless we are willing to do this, Satan will get the advantage. Those are not our words; again they come from Paul (2 Cor. 2:11). Bitterness and discouragement can so overtake one that unless we who are strong in the Lord and aware of the adversary's tactics come to the rescue of one who is overburdened with life's complexities, there is great danger that such a person will not recover but, rather, succumb to despair. It is in these moments that mental derangement can take over to the extent that even a committed Christian can commit suicide.

Suicide has long been a taboo subject that stigmatizes not only the victim but the survivors as well. The act of self-destruction raises vital questions: "Why? Where have I failed?" It is an affront to those who remain, as they anxiously ask, "How can I now face people? What will others think?"

Therefore, those of us who are Christians, when confronted with the fact of suicide—when someone we know has killed himself, or even when we hear of someone we do not know personally who has done this dread thing—it is not our prerogative to sit around speculating on the whys and wherefores. Instead, we must exercise great wisdom, tact, and understanding love that says, "Look, I love you. I don't understand, but I want to be understanding. Your loved one is gone; we entrust him to God's tender mercy. Now what can I do to help you?" Most often just being there, available with love, a comforting arm around the shoulder, and a listening ear will help to ease the pain of the loss and the agony of disturbing questions.

At the outset of creation the Bible tells us, "God saw all that He had made, and found it very good" (Gen. 1:31, *AV*). Life *is* good. Life is to be treasured. How sad when someone despairs of its wonderful possibilities and is driven to suicide. Life is a gift of God, but it becomes really meaningful when love enters the picture. God's great gift to mankind was personified in His Gift of Love, Jesus. When you show to others His Gift of Love, then you give them the greatest gift of all.

If you really want to do something for the world or for someone who has just experienced the loss of a loved one through suicide or for someone who has attempted to take his life but failed, then the thing to do is to reach out with *love*—not the sentimental wishy-washy false brand of giving that poses as love, but genuine *loving* that involves giving of yourself.

3

Suicide: The Whispered Word

If I die I cannot give You glory by praising
You before my friends.
David, the psalmist (Ps. 6:5)

Hope moves a person out of suicidal
preoccupation.
Earl Grollman, Suicide [1]

"Once every minute, someone tries to kill himself. If statistics can be relied upon, some 1,800 people will commit suicide this month alone. Sixty or seventy times a day these suicidal attempts succeed." Karl Menninger has made that statement, which serves to dramatize the seriousness of the problem of suicide. In all probability, however, the actual count of attempted self-murders is higher, since many are not listed as suicides when it cannot be definitely proven that the gunshot, the taking of pills, or whatever, was deliberate. The statistics are staggering, and they are constantly soaring. Suicide is a problem of gigantic size.

Who are these people who are killing themselves or making the attempt? Well, they're not only adults. In 1972, figures stated that twenty million high school students and eight and one-quarter million college and university students in the United States alone headed back to school in the fall. Suicide ranks third as the cause of death among the general adolescent population, which means that from ages fifteen to nineteen the suicide rate is 5.5 per 100,000 for boys and 2 per 100,000 for girls. Among collegians the number is even higher; for every 10,000 college students, 5 to 20 will attempt suicide and 1 to 3 will succeed. Among college students suicide has become the second most frequent cause of death, surpassed only by accidents. Even this count may be inaccurate when you consider that some students kill themselves in what are called "accidents" but are more likely suicides.

Young people are not the only victims of suicide, however. Ralph Barton, one of the nation's top cartoonists, left this note pinned to his pillow before committing suicide: "I have had few difficulties, many friends, great successes; I have gone from wife to wife, and from home to home, visited great countries of the world, but I'm fed up with inventing devices to fill up twenty-four hours of each day."

There are at least two million individuals living in our country like Ralph Barton—individuals who have not found meaning in life and are weary of devising ways to spend their days. But, unlike Barton, these are people who were not successful in their attempts at self-extermination. Some of them are your neighbors, perhaps your husband, wife, or some other close family member.

But the problem becomes even more immense when you read news releases that say the true American suicide rate may be double the reported one! This is true because many attempted suicides are never reported; others, as stated earlier, are listed as accidental.

Women outnumber men in *attempted* suicide by a ratio of three to one. It need not surprise readers that the bored housewife has the greatest suicidal potential. "She makes twice as many attempts as all other female classifications," according to Earl A. Grollman, long involved in family counseling in the state of Massachusetts, in his book, *Suicide*. It is a warning to husbands. Are your wife's needs as an individual being met? Is her life fulfilling?

Positions of leadership and responsibility cause unbearable anxieties for men, leading them to seek an exit from life. Economic recessions, business reverses, and the loss of employment—these have powerful psychological consequences resulting in a higher ratio of *completed* suicides for men than for women. The Los Angeles Suicide Prevention Center reports that the sex ratio for completed suicide is 2.5 men to 1 woman. In the greater Los Angeles area, at the time of this printing, however, the ratio is 1.5 men to 1 woman.

Perhaps the reason is not too difficult to understand. Men tend to take ways that assure success, such as shooting, jumping, or hanging. Women generally use more passive means of self-destruction—sleeping pills, poisons, or gas. A woman wants to look her best even in death, so she is usually not about to blow out her brains with a gun or do something else that might disfigure her in some way; also it is less painful and women shy away from pain. It may sound bluntly cruel to state it that way, but it does happen to be the truth.

Wives need to look to themselves—ask yourself if you are really communicating with your mate? Have you told him (even today) that you love him, that despite problems, financial reverses, loss of his job, or whatever it is that may be weighing him down, you respect and appreciate him? Are you loyally standing by in his time of desperate need or are you demeaning him still more? How tragic if a suicidal death were to shatter your family ties. Ask the widow of a suicide victim!

Both husbands and wives need to communicate with each other. Caught up in the frantic pace of today's living, how many there are who are crying out, reaching out for someone in whom they can confide, someone who will take the time to listen—and love! Marriage is supposed to be a buffer against self-inflicted death, but this is not always the case. Many couples so aggravate each other that one or the other seeks escape through death. Often for religious reasons a couple will not consider divorce. Although divorce is not to be advocated—and divorced men and women are known to have a higher suicide rate than married people— still, in cases where partners are living at continual odds with each other, it would be preferable, it seems, than death by suicide.

Religious beliefs do play an important role in whether a person decides to kill himself or not. The highest suicide rate is known to be among Protestants. Protestants will not like to hear this, but it is nonetheless true. The suicide rate for Jews is lower than the national average, and Catholics also have a lesser incidence of suicide. Perhaps among Catholics this is because suicide is considered by most to be a mortal sin, punishable in the life hereafter. Protestants may have a broader base of understanding regarding the pardoning grace and mercy of the understanding Father-heart of God.

Religious statistics regarding suicides, it has been found, are very difficult to compile. To label a person a Jew, a Protestant, or a Catholic when making a suicide report does not really tell much. How devout was he in practicing Catholicism? How pious a Protestant was she (using the term *pious* in its better con-notation)? How orthodox a Jew was he?

Who commits suicide? People from all races, creeds, and cultural backgrounds. Southern blacks seldom take their lives, but the statistics change drastically in the northern part of the United States. Black males in New York City, for example, from ages twenty to twenty-five, take their lives twice as often as do white men of the same age group. Current documentation in-dicates, however, that suicide among blacks is rising. Some recent studies of the Indian population in this country have uncovered a virtual suicide epidemic among Indian adolescents between fifteen and twenty years of age. This is very sad and surely leads to the observation that the American Indian is deserving of more understanding and respect than he has hitherto received.

Suicide frequency increases with age. This, too, is a sad commentary. Goals have not been attained. Hopes lie unrealized. Marital and family conflicts exist. The middle-aged person who takes a serious look at his life and does not like what he sees in the past and what looms ahead for the future decides that copping out is better than coping. Failure and defeat, tiredness —who needs more of that? It's called "flameout," or the midlife crisis. Aspiration becomes frustration, and suicide is the end result.

Then there are the forgotten elderly. Annually they top the statistics of those whose suicide has been completed. How dreadfully sad and revealing. Even as this is being written, our local evening paper carries the distressing news that an elderly California man shot and killed his wife in their home and then, turning the .45-caliber automatic on himself, committed suicide. This was a murder-suicide pact, not at all an uncommon occurrence among suicide statistics. The couple had left a note citing failing health as the reason. Often the financial burdens, insecurity, terrible loneliness, defects in vision and hearing, and degenerative diseases that make living unbearable contribute to such self-destruction. The forgotten and lonely elderly, feeling useless, unneeded, and a burden to their family or society, choose suicide —death seems better than four walls, no companionship, and the inevitable suffering that accompanies ill health in old age.

An article in *The Church Herald* magazine (May 2, 1970) comments that many people are simply unaware or unthinking in their dealings with those around them, strangely true where young children are involved. Somehow we don't think of a child as being desperate. Yet he can be, and at an early age. For example, a mother and father who were both concerned primarily about their respective careers left the rearing of their four-year-old daughter to a series of impersonal hired persons. One day the little girl said, "I'm going to run away."

Her father told her to go ahead. For a while the child seemed devastated. Finally she said, "You don't love me. I'll eat my aspirin." And she went into the bathroom and swallowed most of a bottle of children's aspirin. After a fast trip to the hospital emergency room, she had her stomach pumped. The parents were warned that this might represent a suicide attempt. They discarded the idea. "She was just trying to get attention," said the father. And he was right. The child was probably trying to get the attention of her parents long enough to assure herself that they loved her. To claim that she didn't understand the finality of death is to avoid the problem.

Young children do wonder whether they are wanted and loved. They need reassurance. They want to hear "I love you" and often. Many times there is a lack of close friendships among children —someone with whom they can share confidences or from whom they can receive psychological support. Many children do not learn the art of cultivating friendships early in life. They are loners not by choice necessarily, but more often because they simply do not understand what goes into the making of being a friend and thereby acquiring friends.

There is a note of encouragement, however, as one considers who it is that commits suicide. Few children do.

There are those still considered children yet old enough to be jailed, who may kill themselves, like the fourteen-year-old whose story was told in the same evening paper that carried the account of the elderly couple mentioned above. This lad, jailed for truancy, hung himself in the same jail where his father committed suicide, in the same way, ten years before. His mother had commented, "I don't know whether I should start blaming people or just sit down and wonder."

However you look at it, whomever it affects—victims and those left behind, who sit and wonder, blaming others and themselves—suicide is tragic for all concerned, tragic and senseless. What is missing in the lives of such as these? Love, caring, and understanding. Did David the psalmist, for example, looking down the corridor of the years and seeing what lay ahead for himself in old age, feel prompted to write, "Cast me not off in the time of old age; forsake me not when my strength faileth (Ps. 71:9, *AV*)"?

Did David, facing feelings of hopelessness and despair, cry out in his soul's distress, "I'm standing here depressed and gloomy; all your waves and billows have gone over me, and floods of sorrow pour upon me like a thundering cataract" (Ps. 42:6a, 7) contemplate suicide? We do not know. We do know, however, that David had great cause for seeking escape, yet David came to his senses time after time. He laid hold upon God's help and cried out,

> But I will meditate upon your kindness. . . . Day by day the Lord pours out his steadfast love upon me, and through the night I sing His songs and pray to God who gives me life. . . . O my soul, don't be discouraged! Don't be so upset! Expect God to act. For I know that I shall again have plenty of reason to praise Him for all that He will do! He is my help! He is my God (Ps. 42:11 and elsewhere)!

David recognized that human life is of value to God even when downcast. Actually, no one is immune from suicidal thoughts. Ask ten different people if they've ever contemplated suicide. They will hedge and hem about giving you an answer, but their very hedging is a clue that the thought has entered their thinking. At one time, as was stated earlier, it was believed that almost all suicides were victims of insanity. There are still those who will insist that if not total insanity, then temporary insanity, propels a person to take his own life. But most studies and most psychologists, psychiatrists, and others who work in the field of suicidology will tell you that the great majority of suicides are in touch with reality; they may be desperate, it is true, but they are normal people. Suicide appears in all ages, in both sexes, on every economic level, and in rural areas, larger cities, and smaller towns.

So *suicide* is the whispered word. Rarely does it make appropriate dinner-time table conversation. It is a kind of taboo topic. Who wants to talk about suicide! But is it right to go on ignoring it as if the problem did not exist when, in fact, it is growing in alarming proportions? The Los Angeles Suicide Prevention Center states that up until ten years ago suicide statistics remained quite stable, but in the last decade there has been a marked change. This should come as no surprise when one considers the times in which we live. Great stress in recent years has been put upon alerting the public to danger signals associated with cancer and heart disease. In the same way, a public conscience alerted to danger signals associated with clues given by the potential suicide could do much to prevent the loss of precious life and salvage a soul. One soul, the Bible tells us, is of infinite worth to the Father.

Psychological studies reveal that before the desperate act of self-execution 75 percent of suicide victims had consulted their family physician, 17 percent had visited a psychiatrist, 7 percent had sought help from a social agency, and 2 percent had taken counsel with either a rabbi, a minister, or a priest.[1]

Not only is it important for the physician, nurse, social worker, and clergyman to be aware of and recognize what may amount to suicidal threats, but each of us also has a responsibility to members of our family and friends to keep the lines of communication open and to demonstrate love. For too long, society has simply condemned suicide. With society becoming more complex, with more people despairing, we need to understand what it is that drives a person to self-murder, and we must take steps to prevent it.

Many communities have established suicide prevention centers; most of the major cities throughout the country have around-the-clock lifelines for potential suicides. Such telephone numbers are advertised in local papers and news sheets where area suicide prevention centers are located. There are known to be over 200 such centers in the United States. A directory of these can be found in the Appendix.

Many churches have stepped into the act, maintaining "Helpline" telephone counseling. Caring individuals in such church and community centers are doing much to sustain life. One such worldwide organization is the Contact Teleministry Movement with fifty-eight functioning centers (at the time of this writing) in this country. A listing of these centers is included in the Appendix to this book. This movement had its beginning in 1966 in Sydney, Australia, based on the work of Dr. Alan Walker at the Central Methodist Mission. Known as Life Line, the movement provides twenty-four hour crisis telephone coverage to everyone in the area. It is an interdenominational organization with church-related telephone centers staffed by well-trained and experienced counselors (most of them volunteers—people who really care). Specifically Christian in approach, according to Executive Director Robert E. Larson, they offer "a place to turn when in despair." Ministering in the name of Jesus Christ to human need, Contact workers are trained to handle a variety of crises, including suicide. What they are doing is holding out hope. It has been proven that hope moves a person out of suicidal preoccupation. Again we look to David. "O Lord," he said, "my only hope is in Your love and faithfulness. Otherwise I perish, for problems far too big for me to solve are piled higher than my head."

Who among us hasn't said something like that! We too are only echoing David's cry. David summed up his second thoughts about death and his problems very well when he said, "For if I die I cannot give You glory by praising You before my friends" (Ps. 6:5).

David had learned what all of us need to understand: We are not promised immunity from periods of despondency, sickness, financial reverses, or problems of one kind or another. But God does exist. He is always there to comfort His own and to make us strong even in our moments of greatest weakness. How does one escape from the kind of despair that drives one to the very brink of suicide? The answer is to be found—and this book will reemphasize that as a basic *fact,* even as Moses, Elijah, Paul, David, and a host of others before us have discovered—and that is to flee to God! It is also *not* a sign of mistrust in God to seek out the help of others highly competent who stand ready with professional know-how.

You say that it's too simplistic, that your situation is so difficult, so distressingly real? So was ours, so was David's and that of the other Bible characters mentioned. But life *is* worth living. Christ says, "Live for Me." It is as we keep our eyes fixed on Jesus that we find meaning in life, even in the midst of the heartache and agony of living, the heartbreak and distress. Then, when God finally does call us to eternity through natural death, *then* there will be meaning in death.

4

Suicide: An Eclipse
in the Soul

by Helen Kooiman

Long, dark shadows had fallen across my
path. Midnight hours, the old-time
Christians called it . . . [a] crisis in my soul.
There was release from my own deep
inner hurt as I . . . laid my wounded spirit
at the feet of God.

Helen Kooiman

He turned my sorrow into joy! . . . so that I
might sing glad praises to the Lord
instead of lying in silence in the grave.

*Psalms 30:11, 12 ***

I was tired beyond the telling, both physically and mentally
exhausted. Every fiber of my being ached; my nerves were taut;
pressure had mounted to the exploding point; and depression had
settled in like a heavy blanketing fog. My usual ability to bounce
back was gone. My vision was obscured by the black pessimism
of despair, and the future stretched before me as one long bout
with loneliness. All I could see was work, loneliness, more work,
and more lonely difficult hours of struggle. Work, loneliness,

* Selected psalms are quoted, from *The Living Bible,* often without reference, through this chapter. The reader is well advised to delve into the
Book of Psalms for himself, using one of the new translations or
paraphrases.

tiredness—the thoughts cycled through my mind in ceaseless repetition. Added to this was the knowledge that most people really didn't understand. Some tried to be understanding, but no one could really comprehend my situation.

In the back of my mind hovered the knowledge that God understood. He cared; He comprehended. But I was so weary of it all. I did not doubt the reality of God, but at the time I needed someone with flesh and bones. I knew all the Bible verses that told me God was a very present help in time of trouble. I shoved them aside. I didn't *want* any more trouble or loneliness. All I wanted was a shoulder to lean on; someone else to help carry the load besides God. I felt starved for love.

I drove thirty-five miles from my home under a mammoth weight of despair, arrived at my destination, and alone, feeling rejected and unwanted, totally incapable of rational thought, reached into the glove compartment of the car and took out the unopened bottle of sleeping pills. There was a can of cola beside me. My last thought was a prayer: "God, forgive me, but I'd rather be with You."

Twelve hours later I awoke in my own bed. Was it a bad dream? A nightmare? But no, I was fully clothed and in my hand was the bottle of sleeping pills, an empty bottle!

I was now a statistic. A living statistic, to be sure, but not so sure that I was glad about it. "You are a walking miracle," the doctor declared. "The pills should have done it; and if they hadn't, the thirty-five-mile freeway drive back to your home certainly should have taken care of your desire to end it all. You couldn't have driven that car back. . . . If I never believed in angels before, I certainly do now. You worked your guardian angels overtime! I have a feeling Someone up there wants you around alive for awhile yet."

I was alive and comparatively well on planet Earth. Now what was I going to do? Had I really wanted a permanent out? Questions, and more questions. There was work to do. Work! I hated the word. But it stared me in the face. Stacks of it. Work is always good therapy, I told myself, and pitched in. Once again I was bouncing. If not very high or with much enthusiasm, at least I was thinking in terms of bouncing and making a slight effort.

Loyal, loving, concerned friends and a very knowledgeable psychologist ministered to me. "Just call me Job, or Moses, or Elijah; maybe Jonah or Jeremiah," I tried laughing, joking somewhat, trying to look at my situation more objectively. A discovery was made: I could still smile, laugh, joke. There had been an eclipse in my soul. Long, dark shadows had fallen across my path. Midnight hours, the old-time Christians called it. I had experienced it. But the sun still rose each morning, the birds still chirped, awakening me, and the day's work was there to greet me. Count your blessings, I reminded myself; work is a blessing, not your bane.

Then I retreated into the psalms. The psalmist became my constant companion. In my copy of *The Living Bible* the Book of Psalms is underlined and circled; there are exclamation points and "Thank you, Jesus," "Yes, Lord," and other little notes, all giving testimony that God had seen and taken me through this crisis in my soul.

> Death bound me with chains, and the floods of ungodliness mounted a massive attack against me. Trapped and helpless, I struggled against the ropes that drew me on to death.
>
> In my distress I screamed to the Lord for his help. And he heard me from heaven, my cry reached his ears . . . he sped swiftly to my aid. . . . Suddenly the brilliance of his presence broke through the clouds. . . . He reached down from heaven and took me and drew me out of my great trials. He rescued me from deep waters. He delivered me from my strong enemy, from those who hated me—I who was helpless in their hands.
>
> . . . the Lord held me steady. He led me to a place of safety, for he delights in me.

I stopped my reading. *"He delights in me?"* Was it really true? *Me?* I read on.

> You have turned on my light! The Lord my God has made my darkness turn to light. Now in your strength I can scale any wall, attack any troop.
>
> What a God he is! How perfect in every way! All his promises prove true. He is a shield for everyone who hides behind him. For who is God except our Lord? Who but he is as a rock?
>
> He fills me with strength and protects me wherever I go. . . .
>
> You have given me your salvation as my shield. Your right hand, O Lord, supports me; your gentleness has made me great. You have made wide steps beneath my feet so that I need never slip. . . . You have armed me with strong armor for the battle.
>
> God is alive! Praise him who is the great rock of protection. He is the God who pays back those who harm me. . . .
>
> He rescues me from my enemies; he holds me safely out of their reach and saves me from these powerful opponents. . . .
>
> Many times you have miraculously rescued me. . . . You have been loving and kind to me and will be to my descendants.
>
> O God, you have declared me perfect in your eyes; you have always cared for me in my distress; now hear me as I call again. Have mercy on me. Hear my prayer.

There followed long periods of prayer where I poured out my heart to the God Who cares for us in our distress, to the God Who is merciful:

> O Lord, hear me praying; listen to my plea, O God my King, for I will never pray to anyone but you. Each morning I will look to heaven and lay my requests before you, praying earnestly. . . . Lord, lead me as you promised me you would. . . . Tell me clearly what to do, which way to turn.

God was at work directing my turning. It was difficult. One does not jump up from trying to go sideways and immediately walk a straight, steady line. I limped, stumbled, struggled. Sometimes I fell down. Then again I would cry out like David:

No, Lord! Don't punish me in the heat of your anger. Pity me, O Lord, for I am weak. Heal me, for my body is sick, and I am upset and disturbed. My mind is filled with apprehension and with gloom. Oh, restore me soon.

Come, O Lord, and make me well. In your kindness save me. For if I die, I cannot give you glory by praising you before my friends. I am worn out with pain; every night my pillow is wet with tears. My eyes are growing old and dim with grief. . . . I am depending on you, O Lord my God.

It was not a misplaced dependence. God could be depended upon to heal the hurting me. Already He was telling me that someday this very book would be written to hold out help and hope to others caught in the web of despair, those for whom life has lost its shadings and all seems very dark and hopeless. When life is black, death does seem the best answer.

It was June 19, 1972, when I wrote in the margin alongside Psalm 4, "Thank you, Jesus." For what was I specifically thanking him this time?

Mark this well: The Lord has set apart the redeemed for himself. Therefore he will listen to me and answer when I call to him. Stand before the Lord in awe, and do not sin against him. Lie quietly upon your bed in silent meditation. Put your trust in the Lord, and offer him pleasing sacrifices. Many say that God will never help us. Prove them wrong, O Lord, by letting the light of your face shine down upon us. . . . I will lie down in peace and sleep, for though I am alone, O Lord, you will keep me safe. .

From one who has been there, you can take it as truth: He is a God Who helps; He is a God Who can be trusted; and He is a God Who keeps us safe. When we are alone, as so many are, He is a Reality, but you must seek Him; you must call out to Him and then reach out and take what He gives. He gives that help through His Word, in that sweet, unexplained Presence that invades your thinking, providing comfort and companionship.

It is when our thoughts are turned inward, so bound up with our problems, loneliness, feelings of self-pity, or whatever it is that is dragging us down, that He cannot get through. It is because we are allowing the enemy of our souls to take over our thinking and we are not doing mortal combat, fighting with the sword of the Spirit, God's Word, as we are told to do. Now this is fact, not mere words that you have read or heard so often before.

What a senseless, tragic waste of life when someone falls to the wiles of the devil through suicide! Such a one could still be standing up, but instead he has slipped out of this world going sideways, which is exactly the expression young people use to describe death by one's own hand.

The Apostle Paul said that our strength could come only from the Lord's mighty power within us (Eph. 6:10), and he was absolutely correct in what he said. Then Paul said to put on all of God's armor so that you will be able to stand safe against all strategies and tricks of Satan. He reminded us that we are not fighting against people made of flesh and blood but against persons without bodies—the evil rulers of the unseen world, those mighty satanic beings and great evil princes of darkness who rule this world, huge numbers of wicked spirits in the spirit world (Eph. 6:11–12). Paul goes on to tell us to use every piece of God's armor to resist the enemy whenever he attacks, and when it is all over, you will still be standing up (Eph. 6:13).

Just what is that armor? As you read this, you may already know. Perhaps you've read it or heard it hundreds of times. Others may be totally unaware of what is needed to wage spiritual warfare—for that is what it is. Paul says we need the strong belt of truth and the breastplate of God's approval. Wear shoes that are able to speed you on as you preach the good news of peace with God. In every battle you will need faith as your shield to stop the fiery arrows aimed at you by Satan. And you will need the helmet of salvation and the sword of the Spirit, which is the Word of God (Eph. 6:14–17).

Finally, Paul says to pray all the time, to plead with God, reminding Him of your needs (Eph. 6:18). I call it "telegram praying." Don't get out of touch with God at any point; keep in constant communication. Save yourself *from* yourself by seeking God's guidance about everything. We are usually our own worst enemy, giving way to self-pity, surrendering to black moods of oppression. We need to take ourselves in hand *and then hand ourselves over to God*. There are times when I say, "Dear God, You are really getting the short end of the deal. I'm such a miserable bargain." Believe me, He doesn't mind.

But it was in the Book of Psalms that I drew closest to God as I came up from that which had plunged me into such despair. David told me that God was my shield Who would defend me; God is a judge Who is perfectly fair. Over and over again the psalmist told me that God is good, *so good*.

David said to this God of goodness, "I cannot understand how you can bother with mere puny man to pay any attention to him!" (Ps. 8:4), and that thought frequently crossed my mind. Out of the fullness of his heart David exclaimed, "O Lord, I will praise you with all my heart, and tell everyone about the marvelous things you do. I will be glad, yes, filled with joy because of you. . . . You have vindicated me, you have endorsed my work, declaring from your throne that it is good" (Ps. 9:1–2, 4).

And to think that I had thought I needed someone else to help me carry the load besides God! Shame engulfed me, remorse for my foolish act. "All who are oppressed may come to him. He is a refuge for them in their times of trouble. All those who know your mercy, Lord, will count on you for help. For you have never yet forsaken those who trust in you" (Ps. 9:9–10).

David told me, "Tell the world about his unforgettable deeds" (Ps. 9:11b). That I would do. That I could do, and so long as God opened doors, I would walk through them using the gifts He had entrusted to me, wasting none of the experiences—sad and glad—that came my way.

> And now, O Lord, have mercy on me. . . . Save me, so that I can praise you publicly . . . and rejoice that you have rescued me. . . .
>
> I will bless the Lord who counsels me; he gives me wisdom in the night. He tells me what to do.
>
> I am always thinking of the Lord; and because he is so near, I never need to stumble or to fall. Heart, body, and soul are filled with joy. For you will not leave me among the dead; you will not allow your beloved one to rot in the grave. You have let me experience the joys of life and the exquisite pleasures of your own eternal presence.
>
> Lord, how you have helped me before! You took me safely from my mother's womb and brought me through the years of infancy. I have depended upon you since birth; you have always been my God. Don't leave me now, for trouble is near and no one else can possibly help.
>
> O Lord, don't stay away. O God my Strength, hurry to my aid. Rescue me from death; spare my precious life. . . . Yes, God will answer me and rescue me.
>
> I will praise you to all. . . . I will testify of the wonderful things you have done. . . . I will say, "Praise the Lord . . . fear and reverence his name . . . for he has not despised my cries of deep despair; he has not turned and walked away. When I cried to him, he heard and came."

The Book of Psalms is lengthy. I identified with all 150 of them. The psalmist's mood fitted mine. He reflected my own spirit. There was release from my own deep inner hurt as I, with the writer, laid my wounded spirit at the feet of God.

Not all of the psalms were penned by David, but they were all derived originally from the blessed Holy Spirit. No wonder there was so much of comfort. But there was more than comfort. There was a balance of that which was instructing my mind as well as encouraging my heart. From the psalmist I learned how to handle the varying moods that ebbed and flowed like the tides, a not uncommon experience of one who has gone through the suicidal crisis. **1824214**

When David said that he felt helpless, overwhelmed, and in deep distress and that his problems seemed to go from bad to worse (Ps. 25:16), I, as a woman, alone, making the adjustment to a new job in a strange community, could feel some of the guilt about my suicide attempt slip away. Here was a man after God's own heart making that kind of a confession. "See my sorrows; feel my pain; forgive my sins. . . . Save me from them! Deliver my life from their power! Oh, let it never be said that I trusted you in vain! . . . Assign me Godliness and Integrity as my bodyguards, for I expect you to protect me and to ransom me from all my troubles" (Ps. 25:18, 20–22).

David lifted his hands to heaven and implored God's help. God did not ignore His servant's cry, and I knew He would help me, too. David, to our knowledge, did not make an attempt on his own life, but he must have felt like it many times. When you are the object of a schizophrenic king's hate (King Saul, whose throne David took), when you are rejected by your countrymen and your favorite son (who tried to usurp your kingdom), when you lose your best friend, when you are faced with marital problems (and David had *many* wives), when you are confronted with your own sins and the magnitude of your own willfulness, when you are charged with the responsibility of having to make grave decisions of far-reaching importance, and when you have to face the death of loved ones, then you, like David, will experience crisis moments and deep anguish. Out of all this, David wrote the psalms.

I plead with you to help me, Lord, for you are my Rock of Safety. If you refuse to answer me, I might as well give up and die.

Oh, praise the Lord, for he has listened to my pleadings! He is my strength, my shield from every danger. I trusted in him and he helped me. Joy rises in my heart until I burst out in songs of praise to him. The Lord protects his people and gives victory to his anointed king.

Thus spoke the psalmist. My heart broke out in songs of praise and I knew that I, too, had been protected by the Lord. He was going to give me victory. "Then he turned my sorrow into joy! He took away my clothes of mourning and gave me gay and festive garments to rejoice in so that I might sing glad praises to the Lord instead of lying in silence in the grave. O Lord my God, I will keep on thanking you forever."

5

Suicide: A Satanic Tool

Have courage for the great sorrows of life,
and patience for the small ones, and
when you have laboriously accomplished
your daily task, go to sleep in peace.
God is awake.
Victor Hugo

Discouragement is a satanic tool that seems
to fit my disposition very well.
*Jim Elliott, martyred missionary to the
Auca Indians in Ecuador, from his journal* [1]

As we read the letters that come into the *Hollywood Free Paper* office, we note a recurring theme. It is one of pessimism and despair, frequently punctuated with the death wish, sometimes relating unsuccessful suicide attempts and sometimes telling of a friend's success in taking his or her own life.

These letters read like this: "I went forward at a youth rally and accepted Christ. But it only lasted a week, after that I became a phony. I've been putting on an act ever since. I cry at night because I'm so lonely. I thought God would fill my loneliness. . . . I wish I were dead." That letter, like so many others, ended with big, bold letters: "PLEASE HELP ME CUZ I NEED HELP!"

In comparison with some of the letters, that one was mild; yet it pointed up a desperate loneliness (see *On Lonely Street with God*).[2] Accepting Christ, contrary to what many young people think, is not like receiving a vaccination that promises future immunity against a certain disease. Although the Bible does give us many promises to which we can cling and which we can claim, we must take the whole counsel of God, and He does tell us that here on earth we will have many trials and sorrows (John 16:33), but the last half of that verse tells us to cheer up, for Jesus has overcome the world.

The letters convey a refreshing honesty, but the feelings of frustration, fear, and failure to understand the Bible come across as being very heavy. Burdensome. Too much of too much. A fifteen-year-old girl wrote,

> I really don't know why I'm writing you when I could go see my pastor or someone else close by. Maybe I don't want to face anybody, or else maybe I'm hoping for some magical words of wisdom that will make my problems vanish and be lost forever. I think my real reason is I'm afraid no one will understand or else they will say there's no hope for me. I guess you could call me a faded Christian.

A faded Christian! A faded Christian? At age fifteen a faded Christian? The letter continued,

> I've never really understood why my Christianity never lasts. It always fades away like everything else. I've gone to Bible studies and really gotten turned on to Jesus and have accepted Him and the whole bit, but please tell me why it never lasted. A few days later I'd be myself again. I was sincere and knew how much I needed Jesus, but each time something was missing.
>
> For over a year I've accepted Jesus over and over again, but something always goes wrong. I don't want Jesus for a day, week, or month, but forever. It never seems to work out that way however. I've asked Christ into my life so many times, but it never lasts. One of these days isn't Jesus going

to get tired of coming into my heart (I know He comes in) and then being rejected? Won't He just leave for good? The last time this happened I realized I was playing games with God. Since then I've made no more attempts to ask Him back in. But I'm so unhappy without Him. I know I need Him, but I just can't be a successful Christian. Maybe it's because I never know if I have the Spirit or not. People told me you either have Him or you don't have Him. . . . Please help me! Please tell me how to be a successful Christian. Tell me how my love for Him can last. I'm so depressed, and it seems each day God gets further away. I've let it go for so long now, unless something happens soon, *I'm going to do something like take my life.* Please be the one to help me find my way back.

It helps to realize that some of the greatest biblical heroes voiced the same type of perplexing feelings, such as David crying out, "Oh, for wings like a dove, to fly away. . . . I would fly to the far-off deserts and stay there. I would flee to some refuge from all this storm" (Ps. 55:6–8).

The Bible does give ample evidence that feelings of uncertainty are not uncommon. It urges upon us, however, the need for patience and faith. Often we hear the term "the impatience of youth," which explains in part the agonizing uncertainty that plagues so many. Anxiety is not of God. Neither is worry. The familiar maxim, "If you worry, you do not trust. If you trust, you do not worry," makes good sense. It is characteristic of the enemy of our souls that he should attack us with worry, defeat, and questions concerning the reality of Jesus' coming into our hearts when we accept and invite Him in. When Satan succeeds, he gets us going sideways, staggering toward defeat. Like ruts in a road that become deeper with usage, doubts such as this girl wrote about in her letter make inroads upon our peace of mind.

Another revealing letter showing similar feelings of doubt reads,

I hope you can help me. My mind is all fouled up and I'm so disturbed I don't know what to do. I'm not on drugs or anything; I'm just terribly depressed and confused. My problem is that I've prayed and prayed for Jesus to come into my heart but I don't feel anything, and I still hurt people's feelings and go to wild parties, etc. I've been trying to reform, but it's really getting me down. Everyone says that they cried their hearts out when they received Jesus. I guess I haven't received Him, because I haven't cried like that. But I want to receive Him more than anything else in the world. I used to believe strongly in the occult until I heard about Jesus. It seems, however, that all the churches around here are stiff preachers preaching to ladies in their Sunday best and everyone sleeps during the sermon.

I want to know for sure if Jesus really loves me. If He does, why can't I seem to accept Him? My grades are dropping because I spend so much time either praying or partying. I really love Jesus, but why can't I accept Him? Please write back or do something. I'm desperate.

The devil, our sworn enemy, is a "murderer from the beginning" according to John's gospel (John 8:44). It is plain to see, as we read letters like this, why suicide is the third leading cause of death among young people between fifteen and nineteen years of age. If Satan succeeds in destroying the younger generation, he has accomplished a mighty aim.

How important it is to recognize that such doubts and questions give evidence that the one so wondering is important to Jesus. Otherwise, why would Satan bother with you? The devil is happiest when he sees that he can destroy one of God's children. It was Jim Elliott, martyred missionary to Ecuador, who wrote in his diary, "Discouragement is a Satanic tool that seems to fit my disposition very well."

The disciple Peter, who knew what it was to be hounded by Satan, said, "Be careful—watch out for attacks from Satan, your great enemy. He prowls around like a hungry, roaring lion, looking for some victim to tear apart. Stand firm when he attacks. Trust the Lord; and remember that other Christians all around the world are going through these sufferings too" (1 Pet. 5:8–9).

The recognition then must come that each one of us is important to Jesus. It is Satan who is planting these seeds of mistrust and doubt in our thinking. Count it a joy and a privilege to be so attacked, but don't succumb to the battle. Fight it. Suffer through it. Peter said, "After you have suffered a little while, our God, who is full of kindness through Christ, will give you his eternal glory. He personally will come and pick you up, and set you firmly in place, and make you stronger than ever. To him be all power" (1 Pet. 5:10–11).

One of the letter writers asks whether God won't get tired of hearing her call out to Him. The answer to that is an emphatic *no*. It is unbelief, pitting circumstances between itself and Christ, that causes doubt and the feeling that Jesus is not there. We are not to count on our feelings, they fluctuate; we are to rest on *the fact* that Jesus does exist, He does come into our hearts when we invite Him, and we do not need constantly to be inviting Him in when He is already there. We need to accept the fact of His abiding presence.

The resources at our disposal are unbelievable. God, the Creator of the universe, is big enough to create and take care of the world and still be interested in you and in me as individual persons. "Let not your heart be troubled; ye believe in God, believe also in me" (John 14:1, *AV*). Jesus made that statement to His disciples at a crucial moment in their lives. They were almost petrified with fear. Desperate despondency, darkest doubt filled their minds. Jesus looked at those anxious disciples, just as He still perceives the inner heart of people today. Jesus knows our souls in adversity. He knows every question, every doubt that plagues your thoughts. Every wound that inwardly bleeds is known to Him. There is no way you can escape from His all-seeing eye.

It was Victor Hugo who said years ago, "Have courage for the great sorrows of life, and patience for the small ones, and when you have laboriously accomplished your daily task, go to sleep in peace. God is awake." Yes, God is awake. The psalmist knew that. He said, "He that keepeth thee will not slumber. Behold. . . . He shall neither slumber nor sleep" (Ps. 121:3–4, *AV*).

When Jesus was talking to His disciples after the Last Supper, He told them some of the things that were going to happen to Him. He washed their feet—imagine, Jesus' taking the place of a servant and bathing the dirty dusty feet of His disciples—and then told them that one of them was going to betray Him. He told them that He was going to be leaving them. It broke their hearts. No wonder they were saddened. It showed on their faces. And that's when He said, "Let not your heart be troubled. You are trusting God, now trust in me" (John 14:1).

Those are words for you, too. For one who is contemplating suicide, who wishes to escape the world about him with its problems and difficult people, Jesus is speaking those words to you also. It is as if He is saying, "If you have invited me into your heart, then let your mind rest itself on that, even though circumstances around you are disturbing and upsetting." His words are meant to convey the idea that we are not to be in a state of confusion or hurry. Rest on Him. Be sensible. Patient. Keep possession of your soul and your mind even though you can't keep anything else. You may lose your job, a loved one may have died, someone may have slandered your name. Whatever is causing you such turmoil, Jesus is saying, *"Believe in God and believe in me. Don't be afraid."*

The happiness of heaven is our eventual destination when we are believers. Although all else around us may seem to fall apart and people may fail us (as they will surely do), Jesus that day set before His disciples the indisputable fact that He was going away to heaven to prepare a place for them and for all those who put their trust in Him. Thomas, remember him? He was called doubting Thomas. He had some questions for Jesus. Jesus answered them. (You can read all about it in the fourteenth chapter of John.) Jesus said, "I'm not just making up answers to your questions. These are answers given to me by the Father who sent me" (John 14:24b, 25).

Grasp hold of the reality of God and don't let go. It is this that will energize and fortify you against every onslaught of Satan, who would seek to destroy you and rob you of your faith. Thank God you are being hounded. Struggle can only make you more patient, sensitive, and godlike when, through God's strength and power, you overcome it.

Remember Job? Everything that meant anything to him had been destroyed, swept away, demolished—even his children. But can't you see him lifting his boil-covered arm to heaven and shouting, "Though he slay me, yet will I trust in him" (Job 13:15a, *AV*)?

Stop looking for God to wave some magical wand that will give you all the answers to your questions and remove all the obstacles and problems. Instead, stand up, get out there in that world that so desperately needs help, and act on your faith, weak as it may be, and then watch God move in response to your first feeble steps for Him. Your destiny and the outcome of this world are terribly important to God. He thought so much of it that He sent His Son Jesus into the world to save it.

You are important to God. To us as believers He has entrusted the task of letting the world know about Him. And we don't do it in our own strength. It was for this reason that He went away —so that He could send the Holy Spirit as our Comforter and ever-present help.

The writer of one letter above said that she was so busy either praying or partying that her grades were dropping in school and she felt desperate because of that and other distressing circumstances. We need to praise God more. Our problems persist as long as we bask in them, feeling sorry for ourselves, all turned inward. In Psalm 56, David complains of his enemies; then, with a resounding note of triumph, he declares emphatically, "In God have I put my trust; I will not be afraid of what man can do to me" (Ps. 56:11, *AV*).

"This one thing I know," David shouts, "God is for me! I am trusting God—oh, praise His promises" (Ps. 56:9, 10)! Then he adds, "Thank you, Lord, for Your help" (vs. 12b). Would the world around you doubt God less if they saw you praising Him more?

Matthew Henry, wise old commentator, said in *Matthew Henry Commentaries*, "Praising and blessing God is work that is never out of season. Nothing better prepares the mind for receiving the Holy Spirit than holy joy and praise. Fears are silenced, sorrows sweetened, and hopes kept up."

"Believe in God," said Jesus. "That doesn't mean protection, and it doesn't mean safety; it doesn't mean security, and it doesn't mean immunity from suffering and conflict," wrote J. Wallace Hamilton. God is not a security blanket. He is much more than that. Hamilton continued,

> This is not a safe and secure world; there is no promise any-
> where that you won't get hurt because you believe—it is the
> other way around. "Behold," said Jesus. "I send you forth as
> sheep in the midst of wolves" (Matt. 10:16, *AV*). "If they
> persecuted me, they will also persecute you" (John 15:20,
> *AV*). But you can face that; you can stand up to anything
> because of God, because you believe in God.[3]

It is not stretching a point to say that every day's mail at the *Hollywood Free Paper* office brings suicidal threats or confessions of suicide attempts. We are thankful that people feel they have in the paper someone on whom they can unburden themselves. One young person, after spelling out her heartache and speaking openly of the despair she felt and how, as a result, she was turning to what she called "escapist pleasures," added as an afterthought, "Oh, I forgot, sorry—you're a business organization and not a crying towel."

But that's not quite the whole truth. Yes, one must operate the publishing of a paper such as the *Hollywood Free Paper* using business principles, but the purpose in being is to give out the message that in God, through Jesus, we have access to "a crying towel." There will be those who will take offense at giving Jesus the label "crying towel," but we have the feeling that He understands. He wants us to give Him our tears, and if readers feel they want to use the *Hollywood Free Paper* and our shoulders to cry on as they reach out for Jesus, then we stand ready to help you reach Him.

There is nothing wrong with tears. One need not be ashamed of shedding them. Many were spilled in the Bible, particularly by the writer of the Book of Psalms. Always, however, the God of all comfort was there with reassurance. At one point David, in great turmoil, cries out, "You have seen me tossing and turning through the night. You have collected all my tears and preserved them in your bottle! You have recorded everyone in your book" (Ps. 56:8).

David, however, was unwilling to "throw in the towel." He may have wept, but he knew God could be depended upon to understand what those tears were all about. David didn't hang up his harp on the willow trees; he didn't unstring it and lay it aside. He kept it and himself right in tune by singing God's praises. He encouraged himself in God; he did not look to people or the circumstances surrounding him. It was God's providence, His power and promises, that David trusted in. God was his confidence.

Just as the blood of the saints, spilled through the years as they have suffered for the cause of Christ, is precious to the Lord, so too the tears we shed as we call out to Him are not wasted. They are not lost to God. The tears of God's people are bottled up and sealed among God's treasures. God will reckon with those who have caused tears to come from His people's eyes. Prayer and tears, David is telling us, are good weapons for God's people as we face that which shakes us to the very roots of our faith.

In many places throughout the Bible we read of God's saying, "I have seen thy tears." We, like the biblical saints who cried to the Lord, need to remember that God answered and delivered His people then from unbelievably harsh circumstances and that He has been doing this down through all the intervening centuries. He is not a God of caprice, answering then and refusing now!

God doesn't hand out medals to those who do not weep! Weeping is a very valid and normal emotion—even for men. God made you with a sensitive nature and the capacity to feel and experience emotions and grief. Remember, the Bible says that even "Jesus wept."

Letters expressing the desire to die and end it all come not only from young people but also, surprisingly, from those well advanced in age. In the same mail with a suicidal plea for help from some young person may come an equally strong plea from a seventy-one-year-old or a middle-aged person. When the young girl wrote that it seemed that all the churches in her area did was have stiff preachers preaching to ladies in their Sunday best, we were moved by her observation but saddened that a gap may exist in some churches between both age groups—and not just an age gap but a love gap.

The young are impatient with the seeming lovelessness of the old, and the middle-aged and old are ignorant of and impatient with youth. Both err. "I am getting nowhere on my own. I need help. I would be better off dead," writes a seventy-one-year-old. Youth needs to understand that little old ladies in their Sunday best need God too. Those more mature in age need to let their thinking react with the kind of sane maturity that shows the love of God that they have long professed to have. Both need to respond to each other with love. There is no other answer. We are to be walking love to each other.

The child who said to his mother, "I want a God with a face on," was not asking for the impossible. He was only expressing what mankind has always sought after—reality. He wanted something definite, something tangible. He wanted a *someone* for a God, not a something.

The letters received by the *Hollywood Free Paper* are from people who, in their own way, are asking for a God with a face on. I wonder if God is not trying to get a message across to each of us. Many have only foggy notions about God. To them He is somewhere "out there"—remote, hazy, beyond time and space. He is unreal. Could this be because they have not seen Him in you or in me? Where has the love in your heart for Jesus carried your concern and compassion for others?

Would your own life be less messed up if you were honestly as concerned about others as you profess to be? They say that an attempted suicide is always a plea for help, and all verbal indications or threats to take one's life should be taken seriously. Look around you. You may have just written a letter stating your wish to kill yourself. Is there someone near at hand who may be feeling the same way although they have not expressed the wish outright? Try giving yourself away—your love, that is—instead of throwing your life away. In the process you may be responsible for salvaging the life of another as well as your own. It's worth a try. You have nothing to lose and everything to gain—a better life here and now and an assured eternity with Jesus.

6

Suicide: The Abyss of Dark Pessimism That Ends in Depression

In the absence of hope faith flounders.
Faith demonstrates to the eye of the
mind the reality of those things that cannot
be discerned by the eye of the body.
Faith is believing where we cannot see,
trusting in Christ beyond the horizon,
believing His goodness beyond our sight,
trusting His word against the optic nerve.

J. Wallace Hamilton,
What About Tomorrow [1]

To suggest that we are to be walking love to others and that for the suicidal individual this suggestion is worthy of implementing immediately is not to offer a simple answer to a complex situation. We are fully aware of the immensity of the problem of suicide. The sociological, psychological, and ecological correlation and the many diverse factors associated with suicide and repeated attempts at suicide are not unknown to us.

We believe, too, that the role of the counselor trained in treating the suicidal individual is an essential part of recovery. In no way would we minimize the help to be received from psychologists, psychiatrists, and therapists, who can delve into the suicidal person's complex physical and psychological makeup. We would emphasize, however, the importance of obtaining the help, whenever possible, of a Christian in such instances.

How our hearts ached when we read the letter from the young person who said that he was a "walking drug store," taking sixteen pills a day and five different drugs, and that he goes to a therapist who does not understand his interest in Jesus People and his professed love for Christ. "I have a private session once a week," the letter stated, "and a group session also once a week. I tried talking to my private therapist about God and Jesus and the questions, problems, and anxieties I've got. But no go! The therapist said, 'I can't treat you and handle your God too.' I shut up then. I always do."

It was a pathetic plea for help, as so many of the letters are. "All of my letter adds up to one big pile of garbage," he stated. "And I don't know how to get any of it out of my life. My life is so rotten, and I want to be clean. I have a really crummy feeling about the way I treat myself and God.

"The beach is beautiful and I walk a lot there, but there are no answers at the beach or in the other walks I take alone. *God, I feel so messed up, and this is something I can't even talk to a 'shrink' about*," he cries out, and you can feel the heavy despair. Then he asks the familiar question, "Is life worth hanging onto anymore?"

Those who have turned their backs on the longhairs and the kids who dress in weird-looking clothes or who wear grubby jeans would do well to take a second look at some of the heartbreaking letters included in this book. In turning our backs on young people like that, we are guilty of sending them into deep depression and many into killing themselves. The letter ended with the question, "I don't know of anyone around here who loves Jesus and can tolerate blue jeans and long hair at the same time. Do you?" and he gives his address, hoping we can direct him to someone in his area who does love Jesus, doesn't mind a person's personal appearance, and can also help him with his depression and questions about God and Jesus.

To those who write such letters we would remind them of John the Baptist. To those who criticize the longhairs and the attire of others we would also point to John and other biblical prophets. We literally cheered when we read what Dr. Kenneth L. Wilson said on the subject in his book, *Have Faith Without Fear*. Dr. Wilson says,

> John the Baptist couldn't keep himself straight. He was a sloppy dresser, ate any old thing, wouldn't work at a respectable job, and lived out among the rocks somewhere. Would you have wanted your daughter to marry John the Baptist? Personally, I wouldn't even have wanted him on my living-room sofa.
>
> But he and other beatniks of the Bible look quite respectable from today's germ-free distance. We've shifted to targets closer at hand. We're now outraged by the very same outspoken, piercing-eye, unconventional performance that we have learned to respect in those other men who have been deodorized by time. Of course, long hair does not a prophet make, or unwashed clothes a saint.[2]

There is enough food for thought in those comments for everyone to take and digest for a long time.

Hopelessness often precedes suicide and is manifested by depression. Depression is frequently mentioned in the letters that relate suicide attempts or express the death wish. A letter will state,

> At this point I've reached an all-time low in my life. My creative drives, ambitions, and human friendliness have seemingly evaporated. I've never felt so alone in my entire life. I feel as though I haven't one friend in the world. Now you're saying, "But Jesus is your friend." I've heard this and all the other Jesus raps many many times. I'd wholeheartedly like to believe these things. I want to accept Christ into my

life so that I might spread joy instead of self-pitying despair.
What can I do? I'm at the end of my rope.

Such depression, it can be seen, is the response to a life situation that is perceived as hopeless. One can see the feelings of incompetence, helplessness, lack of resources, of no paths seemingly open. There are guilt, repressed rage, sadness, and unanswered questions as the person gropes his lonely way through the abyss of dark pessimism that can only end in deep depression and frequently ends in suicide.

Friendship with Jesus, however, which *can* put an end to such deep depression, is not reserved for a chosen few. An honest confrontation with the Christ of the Bible, as revealed in the Gospel accounts, stepping out with even the smallest degree of faith, grasping hold of what one understands, and praying for guidance and *more* understanding will bring the help the suicidal person so desperately craves. More often than not, God will use other people. It is a commonly held belief by those working in the field of suicidology that most suicides can be prevented. Dr. Paul W. Pretzel, writing in his book, *Understanding and Counseling the Suicidal Person,* states, "Anyone in the emotional vicinity of the suicidal person, including family members, clergymen, physicians, therapists, and friends, is in a position to prevent a tragic and wasteful death."[3] The writer of the above letter had a good understanding of her situation, stating that she knew she was too independent and self-assured.

My problem in fully accepting Christ is my lack of faith that He will hear me. I am convinced, however, that He hears other people. But I am totally lost and ready to call it quits. Please, any suggestions will be appreciated. I guess I'm not as self-sufficient as I've thought I've been for the past nineteen years. I want to start a new life. I realize it's never really too late.

And it is not too late. Of the many poems Ogden Nash wrote, one was entitled "Prayer at the End of a Rope." There have been many individuals who have had that "at-the-end-of-the-rope" feeling, who, in their despair, have called out to God in prayer and have been wondrously comforted and helped. Jonah prayed such a prayer from the belly of the whale. But although he is often thought of in this regard, he wasn't the only one that the Bible records who cried out to God when he had reached the end of his rope.

Look at the eleventh chapter of Hebrews. There you will find what is often referred to as "the roll call of faith" chapter. These are people who knew what it was to have the friendship of God and much more. There, faith is defined, as the writer of the book asks the question so many others ask, "What is faith? It is the confident assurance that something we want is going to happen. It is the certainty that what we hope for is waiting for us, even though we cannot see it up ahead. Men of God in days of old were famous for their faith" (Heb. 11:1–2).

Here we are introduced to Abel, Enoch, Noah, Abraham, Isaac, Jacob, Sarah, Joseph, Moses, Rahab the harlot, Gideon, Barak, Samson, Jephthah, David, and Samuel, and mention is made of "all the other prophets" (men who possessed faith).

These people all trusted God and as a result won battles, overthrew kingdoms, ruled their people well, and received what God had promised them; they were kept from harm in a den of lions, and in a fiery furnace. Some, through their faith, escaped death by the sword. Some were made strong again after they had been weak or sick. Others were given great power in battle; they made whole armies turn and run away. And some women, through faith, received their loved ones back again from death. But others trusted God and were beaten to death, preferring to die rather than turn from God and be free—trusting that they would rise to a better life afterwards.

Some were laughed at and their backs cut open with whips, and others were chained in dungeons. Some died by stoning and some by being sawed in two; others were promised freedom if they would renounce their faith, then were killed with the sword. Some went about in skins of sheep and goats, wandering over deserts and mountains, hiding in dens and caves. They were hungry and sick and ill-treated—too good for this world. And these men of faith, though they trusted God and won his approval, none of them received all that God had promised them; for God wanted them to wait and share the even better rewards that were prepared for us (Heb. 11:33–40).

There are many searchers for truth, hungry to discover what faith is, who tell us they were baptized as babies and were brought up in "good Christian homes." Some state that they are confirmed and take communion every month. The mail brings hundreds of letters from young people telling of estrangement from parents within the confines of their "so-called Christian homes." It is a sad commentary when a young person writes to say his home is "a battlefield and I am tired of looking out of windows and crying out to nobody."

It is astonishing and not a little upsetting to read the ages of many of the correspondents. There are an amazing number of thirteen- and fifteen-year-olds who write. A typical letter will start out with "HELP!" in big bold letters. The writer will go on to say, "My parents just say I'm a mixed-up kid. . . . I'm really trying to be someone, so hard in fact that I've even forgotten how to be myself. I'm scared and I think if I can't change or get some help, I don't want to live any longer and I'm thinking of ending it real quick by ODing [taking an overdose of drugs]."

The pleas are made in desperation: "I can't talk to my parents. They just don't understand. But, oh God, am I mixed up! I don't know whether I'm coming or going. Please give me an answer quick!" Another thirteen-year-old, raised in what is supposed to be considered a Christian home, cries out, "I am thinking of putting my hand through a window or slitting my wrist or doing something. I don't think I can go on living like this."

The letters come from every state in the country; the thirteen-year-olds in New York seem to be no different from those in Kansas, Texas, or California. "I'm only thirteen, but I've been searching, unsuccessfully, for an effective relationship and understanding with God and Christ. My faith is so shaky, with all kinds of doubts. I'd like to give God a chance, but if it doesn't work, I'd just as soon call it quits for good."

With insight beyond their years, we cannot help but marvel at the apparent lack of communication between these young people and their Christian parents. "I don't want to get into the 'Sunday Christian' rut my folks are in. I want to get onto the true Christian 'track of life.' Please help me before I pack up and leave home or cop out altogether." There are letters from "preachers' kids," one of whom stated,

> I hesitate to say I'm a Christian, however, because you'd never guess it. I feel so alienated from God, but I want to be close to Him, but I'm so low and unworthy. So many of my "Christian" friends have stepped on me, even some "Christian" adults, and I'm so disillusioned I'm afraid to trust or believe anyone anymore. Lots of people run the "Jesus People" down, but if you are for real, will you please, please write me back and tell me what to do. If you are what you say you are, please don't let me down. I'm depressed and so desperate.

And always there is the question, "What really is faith and how can I have Jesus for my friend?" These are "end-of-the-rope" types of letters that wrench one's heart, coming from those who are without hope. But faith and hope go together, and the same things that are the objects of our hope are the objects of our faith. "Faith demonstrates to the eye of the mind the reality of those things that cannot be discerned by the eye of the body." This is where hope enters the picture, and in the absence of hope it is no wonder faith flounders.

The triumphs of faith in the lives of Hebrew heroes and heroines, as described so dramatically in the eleventh chapter of Hebrews, is powerful evidence that faith is something that is intensely practical. Faith is "taking God at His word." Faith is "accepting as true what God has revealed." When the Bible says that "faith is *assurance* of things hoped for," it must be understood that this "assurance" rests on divine promises. This is not mere speculation or frothy sentiment. Faith to be genuine will act with absolute confidence upon the reality of God as revealed by His Word and the conviction in one's inner spirit.

Faith can have as its starting point the fact that the visible world points to an invisible Creator. "By faith—by believing God —we know that the world and the stars—in fact, all things— were made at God's command; and that they were all made from things that can't be seen" (Heb. 11:3). The first exercise of faith, then, it would appear from chapter 11 of Hebrews, which deals so specifically with faith, is to accept the fact of creation and its Creator.

So you cannot see beyond today. Thank God for His mercy, which doesn't require that your visible eye see beyond the present moment. Life is to be a moment-by-moment walk with God, not a marathon race. You don't know what the night will bring, but you can trust Him Who made both the day and the night. John Alfred Brashear, lensmaker and astronomer, wrote for his and his wife's gravestone, "We have loved the stars too fondly to be fearful of the night." [4] That's living in the now. This moment is all we've got, and we *can* have faith without fear.

Why is the light of faith so often dim? J. Wallace Hamilton, an imaginative, compassionate preacher now with the Lord, used to answer that query by stating, "If you want to believe, you have to stand where the light is shining." [5] If you want faith, go where other men and women have found it and expose yourself with some measure of regularity to the contagion of other people's faith.

This means that one does not absent himself from fellowshipping with other believers. This means that one goes to the light of the Word. Hamilton calls Thomas, one of the disciples, the spiritual ancestor of the absentee, the man who wasn't there, the patron saint of a whole generation of Thomases living in a fog, wanting more faith. Why? Because they have detached themselves from the Christian fellowship, the community of Christians who can be walking love and the means God often chooses to use to help us in our pilgrimage here on planet Earth.

Thomas was not with Jesus' other disciples that night in the upper room when Jesus presented Himself to them where they had assembled in fear. It was after His crucifixion, after His bodily resurrection.

> The disciples were meeting behind locked doors, in fear of the Jewish leaders, when suddenly Jesus was standing there among them! After greeting them, he showed them his hands and side. And how wonderful was their joy as they saw their Lord!
>
> He spoke to them again and said, "As the Father has sent me, even so I am sending you." Then he breathed on them and told them, "Receive the Holy Spirit. If you forgive anyone's sins, they are forgiven. If you refuse to forgive them, they are unforgiven."
>
> One of the disciples, Thomas, "The Twin," was not there at the time with the others. When they kept telling him, "We have seen the Lord," he replied, "I won't believe it unless I see the nail wounds in his hands—and put my fingers into them—and place my hand into his side."
>
> Eight days later the disciples were together again, and this time Thomas was with them. The doors were locked; but suddenly, as before, Jesus was standing among them and greeting them.
>
> Then he said to Thomas, "Put your finger into my hands. Put your hand into my side. *Don't be faithless any longer. Believe*" (John 20:19–27). [Authors' italics]

What was Thomas's response? Immediate belief. Up until that moment Thomas brooded in lonely solitude, burying his despair in hopelessness. His unbelief and lack of faith reached a terrible climax. He was gripped by the obsession that he could not possibly believe these wild tales that Jesus was alive and had appeared to the disciples unless he could see it for himself. He thought he had to see to believe.

> More than half the world is Thomas, afraid to believe. Half of every human heart is Thomas. . . . A man is at fault in his unbelief when, like Thomas, he stands in his own light; when he won't come where the light is; or when he won't expose his mind to the light. Look at him—this chronic doubter. . . . Thomas, one of the twelve, was absent when Jesus came (the first time). The man who missed the moment missed the Lord. Thomas lived for a week in the shadows of dark despondency, because he wasn't in the place where he was most likely to meet the Lord.[6]

How does a person move from unbelief to belief? From faithlessness, like Thomas, to faith? From the shadows of suicide to the light?

We cheat ourselves because we react negatively in unbelief to emotional doubts that cloud the horizon. Our insistence on facts regarding this thing called faith and belief, when in many other matters we believe even when we can't see, corrodes our thinking with dark fears. How grateful we should be for our amazing five senses. They tell us much, these little gateways through which the physical world invades our consciousness. Yet there is so much unseen that is real and utterly beyond our sensory perception. Hamilton gives a particularly apt illustration that confirms this. He says:

> The world, scientists say, is made of atoms. What do they mean, atoms? Show us some; let us see an atom. We don't see atoms; we believe in them. We believe in what we can't see. And men who couldn't see an atom, split it. We can't

see energy, gravity, electricity—the invisible link between cause and effect. How many things we believe with confidence which we never expect to see at all. We have never seen an idea, felt a truth, or put our finger on a thought. The whole world of the mind, almost everything that is basic in personality—all of it is invisible to our eyes as God is invisible.

So people to whom seeing is believing—who don't believe until they can touch and see—are in a bad way; they live in too small a world; more than that, they live in a deceptive world. Thomas thought that at least he could trust his senses; what he could see and touch, he could believe. But we have learned how deceptive the senses are and how little they can grasp and how much insight it takes to get back of the way things appear to the way they actually are. Our senses fool us, even in small things. To us this desk is solid, but the scientist says it isn't—it is nothing but empty space with electrons whirling around, structured to appear solid. Our eyes tell us that the world is flat, but we know it isn't; that the sun rises, but we know it doesn't; and that the sky is blue; but the color is only optical illusion. Even the beautiful redness of the rose is not real, only a delightful deception of the optic nerve. You can't trust your senses. They don't tell you the whole truth about anything.[7]

Hamilton reminds us that we need to remember that our senses are not adequate; they cannot grasp enough of anything to give us the whole truth about it. He uses the illustration of a ship sailing out to sea and off there, on what we call the horizon, it disappears—it's gone. The horizon isn't real; it's only the limit of our vision, the place beyond which our sight cannot go. If we could only see a little farther, we would know the truth, that the ship is just as big and just as real as when it left the harbor.

Hamilton goes on to explain, *"Well, that is our faith. We believe where we cannot see. We trust in Christ beyond the horizon. We believe His goodness beyond our sight. We trust His word against the optic nerve."* [8] [Authors' italics]

That is our answer, too, for the doubting Thomases today.

for those inclined to feel like throwing in the towel and calling it quits. Jesus said something that day to Thomas about you and me—yes, about us. Jesus told Thomas, "You believe because you have seen me. But blessed are those who haven't seen me and believe anyway" (John 20:29).

We have not seen Jesus or touched Him. We have not heard Him speak in an audible voice even though we claim He answers our prayers. Have you seen Him, heard Him, or touched Him? "The things which are seen," said the Apostle Paul, "are temporal; but the things which are not seen are eternal" (2 Cor. 4:18, *AV*).

Paul's answer to the person who is filled with doubts and despairing of life is this: "Do not look at what you can see right now, the troubles all around you, but look forward to the joys in heaven which you have not yet seen. The troubles will soon be over, but the joys to come will last forever" (2 Cor. 4:18).

7

"Do Thyself No Harm"

> We are in the monsoon and we must
> weather it out. Instead of pining for calmer
> days, the way of wisdom is to learn to
> live . . . wisely and well in the midst
> of continuous strain.
>
> *Dr. Elton Trueblood*

> "Glory in Tribulations." Now, Brudder,
> G-L-O-R-Y don't spell GROWL.
>
> *Sophie, the scrubwoman*

"Please read my letter as if my life depended on it," which indeed it did, for the letter was another written out of sheer desperation. "I have these terrible sinking feelings and my mind is filled with doubts and questions: What if there isn't a God? What if Christianity is a hoax? The time has come to ask for help."

Only in the light of eternity will we ever understand the riddles of this present time. There has never been a time, however, when God's people didn't pass through tempest and storm, but even then there can be light, and there has been, as evidenced in the lives of those recorded in biblical history. The label "doubting Thomas" stuck to Thomas as though it were glued to him, but even that is for our benefit and encouragement. Here was one of the intimate twelve who was plagued with doubts and questions. God saw to it that his doubts were resolved, and He will do the same for today's doubters.

From the doubting Thomas mind let us take a leap of faith and look at the mind of Paul. Paul's reply to one who cried out in desperation, ready to take his own life, was a loud yell, "Don't do it! Do thyself no harm" (Acts 16:28, *AV*). That yell reverberates with a compelling urgency to all those who write or say, "I'm now hanging to my last bit of life and mind. I can't hack this life anymore. I've tried everything from drugs to suicide four different times. Now I'm seeing a psychiatrist, but he can't understand me. Nobody can answer my questions. I've asked dozens of people. Why hasn't God given someone to love me? Why do I get slapped down all the time? Where is happiness? Why aren't my needs filled? Why can't I be content like other people? If God knows me inside and out, and knows what I need, why doesn't He do something about it? How long must I wait? Forever? Please give me the right answers. PLEASE! PLEASE!"

One of the things a vital faith does for us is to reconcile in our thinking the love of God with the severity of the trials and the conflicts we are called upon to endure. There is simply no way any one of us can escape the reality of difficulty and the inevitable fact that life is not going to be all tranquility, stability, and peace. There can be inner stability, inner tranquility, and inner peace, but we are living in tense times, and most of us had better come to terms with the strong probability that we shall live the rest of our days in a time of testing, trouble, and anxiety. Dr. Elton Trueblood stated in one of his books, "We are in the monsoon and we must weather it out. Instead of pining for calmer days, the way of wisdom is to learn to live . . . wisely and well in the midst of continuous strain."

A well thought-out faith rests on the assurance that the future belongs to God, and so even though life seems all lopsided and the balance doesn't weigh in your favor, like the old-time prophet Isaiah, you can say, "In quietness and confidence shall be my strength" (adapted from Isa. 30:15).

The much-respected Dr. Harry A. Ironside, the great Bible expositor, in speaking of rising above one's circumstances, living above the trials, and still rejoicing through them, all the while glorying in tribulations, used to tell the story of a preacher by the name of H. B. Gibbud. One morning, when he was feeling depressed and gloomy, there was a knock on his study door. On opening the door, he saw a raw-boned, unprepossessing-looking woman, who said to him, "Brudder Gibbud, I am Sophie, the woman God called to scrub and preach."

"Oh, yes," said Preacher Gibbud, "I have heard of you." Anyone who attended the old Fulton Street prayer meetings years ago would remember her. Dr. Ironside related how he himself had met her. She was a poor illiterate woman who made her living scrubbing floors in office buildings in lower New York City. But Sophie was a radiant Christian with a tremendous love for Christ. It was she who, with her washboard, sent a missionary to the field when the missionary boards had turned him down.

That day Sophie spoke up to Mr. Gibbud and said, "Brudder, the Lord has sent me to preach to you. This is my text—'Glory in Tribulations.' Now, Brudder, G-L-O-R-Y don't spell GROWL." The minister's face lit up while Sophie went on preaching to him. It was the beginning of a new and glad day of victory for the minister.

Dr. Ironside goes on to ask how many have learned that lesson? It doesn't take much character, or much Christianity, to be happy and content when having our own way and when everything goes the way we want it to go. *But*, when everything goes wrong, to glory in our tribulations, that is something else. To rejoice instead of growling, complaining, and asking why spells victory.

Demon possession is a very real thing. Demons are powerful beings operating in the spiritual sphere all around us. The occult with its mysteries has always appealed to unwary individuals anxious for supernatural help. Thus it is that once again today we are seeing people dabbling in the occult and in magical arts, flirting with demonism. These people can become so enslaved that self-destruction is often one of the disastrous consequences.

Demonism existed in the Apostle Paul's day, too. In Acts there is the story of a demon-possessed girl who was a fortune-teller and earned much money for her masters (Acts 16:16). In the name of Jesus Christ Paul commanded the evil demon to come out of the woman, and it did leave her. Now that the demon was gone out of the woman, she could no longer bring in the money for her masters, and they were indignant. In a rage they grabbed Paul and his companion Silas and dragged them before the judges at the marketplacc (Acts 16:19).

False accusations were brought against the two men by the gathering mob. The judges ordered Paul and Silas stripped and beaten with wooden whips. "Again and again the rods slashed down across their bared backs; and afterwards they were thrown into prison. The jailer was threatened with death if they escaped, so he took no chances, putting them into the inner dungeon and clamping their feet into the stocks" (Acts 16:23–24).

Can you picture that scene? They had been brutally whipped, and now, bruised and lacerated, they were handed over to a jailer, a man so debased in his thinking that without any emotion or any care for their suffering he took the two men and thrust them into the innermost part of the deadly dark dungeon and clamped their feet in stocks. Then he chained, locked, and bolted the doors behind him. Having done all that, the jailer fell asleep.

Did Paul and Silas start questioning, "God, why don't you give someone to love us instead of this kind of treatment? God, why do we get beaten like this? Why all this slapping around? Where is happiness? God, You aren't fulfilling all our needs. This isn't very satisfying. If You know us inside and out and know what we need, why don't You do something about our situation? How long must we endure this kind of treatment?"

God does not object when we come to Him with our doubts and questions or when we turn to others to whom He has made Himself known and voice our doubts to them. We are to encourage and help one another. Voicing our doubts and getting our questions out into the open is one way to get answers. But now listen to the way Paul and Silas responded to *their* harsh treatment by the Roman magistrates.

The Bible tells us that after all this happened:

> Around midnight, as Paul and Silas were praying and singing hymns to the Lord—and the other prisoners were listening—suddenly there was a great earthquake; the prison was shaken to its foundations, all the doors flew open—and the chains of every prisoner fell off! The jailer wakened to see the prison doors wide open, and assuming the prisoners had escaped, he drew his sword to kill himself. But Paul yelled to him, "Don't do it! . . . We are all here" (Acts 16:25–28).

Dr. Ironside says this was the first sacred concert ever held in Europe. "Just two artists, the concert hall just a dungeon; yet these two artists had such effect that they brought down the house! Soon the whole prison began to shake. That was the most successful sacred concert I have ever heard of!" [1]

That may be stretching a point a bit, but for two bleeding and bruised prisoners confined to an inner dungeon, which you can be sure was an unsanitary, dark, and awful place, to be singing songs at midnight in the face of more suffering, humiliation, and possible death was an amazing thing.

I am sure that as Paul and Silas considered their situation, they remembered the One Whom they had set their minds and hearts to follow—Jesus Himself, who was first scourged, humiliated, and then crucified. They expected the same; they counted it all joy that they should be considered worthy to suffer likewise for the cause of Christ. They would not complain or cry out in pain, but they purposed to pray together, seeking God's support and comfort, praying that their suffering for Him might turn others to the furtherance of the Gospel and belief in Christ. They prayed for forgiveness for those who had so ill-treated them. Indeed, it makes no difference to God from where our prayers ascend. There is no place or time that is amiss for prayer, where one's heart cannot be lifted up to God. Can we not learn that there is no reason for dark despair when we belong to Christ?

Certainly a prison at midnight is a most unlikely place and time for someone to be praying, singing, and praising God. Yet that is precisely what Paul and Silas did after their prayers were concluded. First they prayed, and then they sang praises to God. If anything is liable to put one's voice and heart out of tune, it seems to us that it would be to find one's self in the situation Paul and Silas were in. But no! They praised God that they were counted worthy to suffer shame for His name.

In many places throughout the Bible we are told that this is what we should do in the midst of our trials. David, the sweet psalmist of Israel, in particular, urges that this is a good thing to do. I have to agree with Dr. Ironside and others who believe that if there were more joy in tribulation, more triumphing in trouble in our own day, we would see more shaking by the power of God.

> The world is watching Christians, and when they see Christians shaken by circumstances as they themselves, they conclude that after all there is very little to Christianity; but when they find Christians rising above circumstances and glorying in the Lord even in deepest trial, then even the unsaved realize the Christian has something in knowing Christ to which they are strangers.[2]

This is what happened to the Philippian jailer. The shock of the earthquake awoke him; he may even have been awakened earlier by the singing of Paul and Silas, but certainly the earthquake jarred him into action. Startled awake, hearing the cries of the prisoners, "Hey, my chains are loosed" and "My feet, my feet, I can lift them out of the stocks," and others joyously crying out as, with surprise, they make the discovery that they are no longer bound, the jailer springs to his feet. Not only were the prisoners exclaiming in surprise, but the jailer suddenly saw that the prison doors were flung wide open, and he assumed that the prisoners were shouting to each other as they made their escape. But no! Just as he reached for his sword, ready to kill himself, from out of the dungeon he heard the yell, the warning cry of Paul, "Don't do it! Do thyself no harm! We are all here" (Acts 16:28).

Under Roman law the jailer was responsible for these prisoners. Should he lose even one of them, he would have to pay for it with his own life. Such a payment would have meant a terrible death, an ignominious death by Roman executioners who would show no mercy.

This was a time in history when philosophers allowed and even often advocated self-murder. Roman Stoicism is full of exhortations to suicide. The most famous such precept is Seneca's:

> Foolish man, what do you bemoan, and what do you fear? Wherever you look there is an end of evils. You see that yawning precipice? It leads to liberty. You see that flood, that river, that well? Liberty houses within them. You see that stunted, parched, and sorry tree? From each branch liberty hangs. Your neck, your throat, your heart are all so many ways of escape from slavery. . . . Do you enquire the road to freedom? You shall find it in every vein of your body.[3]

Seneca himself stabbed himself to death to avoid the vengeance of the Roman emperor Nero, who had once been his pupil. There was no gap between rhetoric and reality. The many writers of the day, the philosophers, a great company of distinguished men of the ancient world, as well as slaves and the common man and woman, died by suicide in the Roman fashion. "To live nobly also meant to die nobly and at the right moment. Everything depended on the dominant will and a rational choice," according to the writer A. Alvarez in his masterful study of suicide, *The Savage God.*[4]

Thus, Paul was prepared for what the jailer might do. Alvarez calls it "icy heroism," indicating an extraordinary inner discipline —a discipline of the soul that they did not believe in. "But it also says something about the monstrous civilization of which they were a part. . . . Stoicism, in short, was a philosophy of despair."[5]

Paul cried out loudly not only to make the jailer hear but also to make him heed. Is there someone reading this book, utterly disheartened, for whom life is a burdensome miserable existence and who is contemplating suicide? Paul's cry is for you also. *"Do thyself no harm! Don't do it!* There is hope and help for you. All is not hopeless. You are of infinite importance to God and, yes, to others around you. Although you feel you are sinking and your mind is filled with doubts and questions, there is a God Who loves and wants to care for you. Christianity is not a hoax. Jesus is real."

8

"Don't Give Up and Quit"

> God has reserved to Himself the right to determine the end of life, because He alone knows the goal to which it is His will to lead it.
> *Dietrich Bonhoeffer, theologian*

God is not an absentee omnipotent Who can't be bothered with the cries of wounded, wondering, despairing people. The Philippian jailer learned this in his moment of panic. He heeded Paul's outcry, and in response,

> Trembling with fear, the jailer called for lights and ran to the dungeon and fell down before Paul and Silas. He brought them out and begged them, "Sirs, what must I do to be saved?"
>
> They replied, "Believe on the Lord Jesus and you will be saved, and your entire household."
>
> Then they told him and all his household the Good News from the Lord. That same hour he washed their stripes and he and all his family were baptized. Then he brought them

up into his house and set a meal before them. How he and his household rejoiced because all were now believers (Acts 16:29-34).

His own fear and sense of need resulted in the conversion of the jailer; not only he but his whole family believed as well. To the panic-stricken heart, whoever or wherever it may be, the answer to the question "What must I do?" is the same. It is simple belief in the Lord Jesus that saves a person not only from the present moment of difficulty but also from all hours of duress and wondering in despair.

That episode actually launched the beginning of the Christian movement in Europe as far as Paul was concerned. The next morning Paul and Silas were set free. Perhaps someone reading this now will be set free, even as the jailer was from the bonds, stronger than the actual chains that had bound the prisoners, that had kept him under such subjection.

The jailer and his family became converts to Christianity, and one can be almost certain that there were many times that followed when they, too, knew what it was to encounter the hatred and persecution of those opposed to the cause of Christ. Then they must surely have remembered Paul and Silas and their prison experience, reminding themselves that when the day is darkest and the prison bars seem firmest, then is the time for praying, singing, and praising God.

A letter postmarked from the state of Virginia reveals the writer's release from the bondage that held her captive for so long: "Now I guess Jesus is just putting me through trials to make me stronger and more resistant to the devil." She was another who had contemplated suicide before coming to the "light" of the Gospel.

The Apostle Paul explained it so well:

If the Good News we preach is hidden to anyone, it is hidden from the one who is on the road to eternal death.

Satan, who is the god of this evil world, has made him blind, unable to see the glorious light of the Gospel that is shining upon him, or to understand the amazing message we preach about the glory of Christ, who is God. We don't go around preaching about ourselves, but about Christ Jesus as Lord. All we say of ourselves is that we are your slaves because of what Jesus has done for us. For God, who said, "Let there be light in the darkness," has made us understand that it is the brightness of his glory that is seen in the face of Jesus Christ.

But this precious treasure—this light and power that now shine within us—is held in a perishable container; that is, in our weak bodies. Everyone can see that the glorious power within must be from God and is not our own (2 Cor. 4:3–7).

Paul's teachings about the necessity of not giving up and quitting, of getting up again, were terribly important to the infant early Church. Persecution of the Christians was widespread; life was unspeakably cruel. When they faced the possibility of being burned alive, beheaded, roasted on gridirons, hacked to pieces, flung from cliffs, or thrown to the lions for sport, many chose self-inflicted death as an alternative. Alvarez says the Stoic calm of the Romans was easily assimilated into the religious hysteria of the early Church. He maintains that Christianity, which began as a religion for the poor and rejected, took the blood lust (of the Roman Stoics), combined it with the habit of suicide, and transferred both into a lust for martyrdom. The Romans may have fed Christians to the lions for sport, but they were not prepared for the Christians welcoming the animals as instruments of glory and salvation. Martyrdom was a Christian creation as much as a Roman persecution.[1]

But even before Christianity began to flourish, the Jews, knowing when capture by the Romans was inevitable, often committed mass suicide rather than fall into the hands of the enemy. References to this are found in the Books of Maccabees (165 B.C.–A.D. 37). Each relates to martyrdom.[2]

Later, in what was called the Talmudic times (A.D. 200–500), suicides were recorded with increasing frequency. Now, however, a condemnatory tone is introduced for the first time. Although considered a crime against God, suicide could sometimes be explained away, understood, and forgiven. But it was not to be encouraged as an act of courage, and the victim was not to be regarded as a martyr.[3]

The prevailing attitude of the era when Christianity first came on the scene among the Stoics, the Cynics, the Cyrenaics, and the Epicureans was that suicide was acceptable, particularly when persecution made life unbearable. Alvarez explains that "To the Romans of every class, death itself was unimportant. But the way of dying—decently, rationally, with dignity and at the right time—mattered intensely. Their way of death, that is, was the measure of their final value of life." [4]

A close look at the writings of the Apostles and the Gospels in the New Testament shows only indirect reference to suicide, and then it is a report of Judas' death (Judas who betrayed Christ). Although Paul urged the Philippian jailer to do himself no harm, for suicide was not the way out of his plight, and although the Apostle's writings are liberally sprinkled with exhortations never to give up, the word "suicide" itself and the act are not mentioned.

But the teaching that God-given life is a mystery and a beautiful gift is prominent. At the very outset of creation, as stated elsewhere, the Bible records that "God saw all that He had made, and found it very good" (Gen. 1:31a, *AV*). Other translations and paraphrases say "it was fitting, pleasant, excellent—and God approved of what had been made completely." This is a thesis that has stood the test of time. *Life is good*. It is to be emphasized that we are not to despair of its possibilities even though today may look very black. Situations change. People change. Paul said:

Our troubles and sufferings are, after all, quite small and won't last very long. Yet this short time of distress will result in God's richest blessing upon us forever and ever. So we do not look at what we can see right now, the troubles all around us, but we look forward to the joys in heaven which we have not yet seen. The troubles will soon be over, but the joys to come will last forever (2 Cor. 4:17–18).

That is a message worth repeating to one's self to fortify the inner man against the onslaughts of our enemy, the devil.

According to Dr. Pretzel, "Most people who are suicidal are intensely suicidal only for a short period of time, and this is usually in reaction to a specific newly introduced stress or rejection. The suicidal crisis may last only for a few hours, and if the victim can survive during this period of time he may never be suicidal again." [5]

Alvarez, in researching his study of suicide, concluded that

The early Christians showed this same indifference to death [as the Romans] but changed the perspective. Viewed from the Christian Heaven, life itself was at best unimportant; at worst, evil: the fuller the life, the greater the temptation to sin. Death, therefore, was a release awaited or sought out with impatience. In other words, the more powerfully the Church instilled in believers the idea that this world was a vale of tears and sin and temptation, where they waited uneasily until death released them into eternal glory, the more irresistible the temptation to suicide became. Even the most stoical Romans committed suicide only as a last resort; they at least waited until their lives had become intolerable. But for the primitive Church, life was intolerable whatever its conditions. Why, then, live unredeemed when heavenly bliss is only a knife stroke away? Christian teaching was at first a powerful incitement to suicide. [6]

The teaching of many of the early church fathers became so extreme that the Church eventually declared them heretics. It was Augustine (A.D. 354–430) who strongly denounced suicide as a sin. He asserted that "suicide is an act which precludes the possibility of repentance, and it is a form of homicide and thus a violation of the Decalogue Article, 'Thou shalt not kill.' "

Augustine's reference is to the sixth of the Ten Commandments, "Thou shalt not kill." His teaching was plain: The man who killed himself broke this commandment and became a murderer. That is a sin. A man can be saved by seeking God's forgiveness from sin and claiming the finished work of Christ on the Cross, but how can a dead man repent? Augustine argued that since life is the gift of God, everything that happens to us, even our sufferings, is divinely ordained and not to be shortened by one's own actions. We are to bear patiently whatever God wills for our lives. To take one's own life, he maintained, was not to accept divine will.

Augustine was a powerful early Church figure, and his arguments were listened to with respect. Largely because of him the door for escape from this life—suicide—was slammed shut. "The decent alternative of the Romans, the key to Paradise of the early Christians, had become the most deadly of mortal sins." [7]

In the eleventh century, another towering Church figure, Saint Bruno, was to come along and call suicides "martyrs for Satan," which left no room for doubt about what he and others like him thought of the act.

Two centuries later, Saint Thomas Aquinas, another strong voice in Church history, opposed suicide on the basis of three powerful postulates: (1) It was against the natural inclinations of preservation of life and charity toward the self; (2) It was a trespass against the community; and (3) It was a trespass against God, who had given man life.

In the long superstitious centuries between Augustine and Aquinas, suicide became the most mortal of Christian sins. Many self-murderers were denied funeral rites and respectful burial in what was considered holy ground. Now we can look back and see the progression of thought: Suicide at first was regarded by many Christians as an act to be tolerated, later it was admired and the person was regarded as some kind of martyr, and then it became the object of intense moral revulsion.

In the seventeenth century, new philosophical currents of thought began to sweep through the Christian Church. John Donne, it is believed, was one of the first to start a chain reaction against the prevailing attitudes of the Church toward suicide. Suicide, up until then, had been labeled as unclean, damned, and degraded. Donne wrote the first English defense of suicide, *Biathanatos. A Declaration of that Paradoxe, or Thesis, That Self-homicide is not so naturally Sinne, that it may never be otherwise.*

Donne wrote about suicide because he himself was tempted to it. He was a masterful writer, but this book was considered one of his less appealing writings. Later it was to become a source of embarrassment to him, when he became the most famous and seductive preacher of his day. It was written in the context of depression. Alvarez wonders if it didn't begin as a prelude to self-destruction and actually finish as a substitute for it. "That is, he set out to find precedents and reasons for killing himself while still remaining Christian—or, at least, without damning himself eternally. But the process of writing the book and marshaling his intricate learning and dialectical skill may have relieved the tension and helped to reestablish his sense of his self." [8] And one might add, his sense of God and divine will.

In the case of John Donne, his Christian training and devotion, like his intellectual energy, were ultimately stronger than was his despair. Donne finally negotiated his middle-life crisis by taking holy orders instead of his life. Donne, like others before and after him and like the Philippian jailer, heeded the Apostle Paul's cry, "Don't give up and quit!"

9

Suicide and Me,
Myself, and I

The suicidal person places his psychological
skeleton in the survivor's closet.
E. S. Schneidman,
Essays in Self-Destruction [1]

Suicide is an insult to humanity.
Immanuel Kant

Try the Savior's side instead of suicide.
"First Mate Bob" (Paul Myers)
founder of the Haven of Rest Broadcast

Suicide signifies a veiled attack upon others.
By an act of self-destruction, the suicide
hopes to evoke sympathy for himself
and cast reproach upon those responsible
for his lack of self-esteem.
Earl A. Grollman, Suicide [2]

Death before dishonor and suicide for love has been a popular
theme among poets and playwrights for centuries. On paper or
on the stage, the suffering of a tragic hero or heroine who ends
up taking his or her own life is often made to appear somewhat
noble, but in actual life there is nothing grandiose about the
act at all. It has been said that suicide is ugly for onlookers,
devastating for relatives, and harrowing even for those profes-
sionally involved. Anyone who has been at all close to a suicide

situation knows it is impossible to come away remaining aloof and unfeeling.

Death is a robber. That fact cannot be denied. So death by suicide brings the greatest of all affronts to those who remain. Often this was the intention of the one who took his or her own life. Selfish motives were involved—feelings of self-pity, strong narcissistic tendencies, self-love; that is, excessive interest in one's own appearance, comfort, importance, abilities, and the like. Yet even such as these need help. It is shocking that most preventable suicide is such a tragically childish act, often a way of seeking attention or sympathy. "The suicidal person places his psychological skeleton in the survivor's closet." In so doing, the suicide derives satisfaction from the thought that he can make those who hurt him or denied him in some way, whether it was real or imagined, live with the memory for the rest of their lives that they were, in fact, the cause of his killing himself. He wants them to live with guilt, shame, and self-blame.

Presuicidal communications and conversations, as well as suicide notes, give many clues as to the "why" of suicide. There are those who take their own lives who are selfish manipulative-type individuals who, when they cannot have their own way, will resort to self-murder or make an attempt upon their own lives to gain attention and sympathy. Many such persons take just enough drugs, for example, to put themselves into a stupor and will time their attempt to coincide with someone's coming home from work or an expected visit. They know they will be discovered "in time." Sometimes, however, this is not the case, and in their stupefied condition they may go on to take more drugs, forgetting the actual count, and end up a suicide statistic. Their little scheme has backfired, and death is the result.

Still, such as these are to be pitied. Christian love requires that we not withhold love even from those who are unlovable for one reason or another. We should do what we can to help them and to secure professional help to see them through their crisis times.

But would a Christian do that? Is it possible for a Christian to be guilty of resorting to such means to get attention or to try to regain back a lost love? The answer is yes. An editorial in the magazine *Christianity Today* stated, "While a strong Christian commitment tends to reduce the possibility of suicide, it does not eliminate it." [3] These are individuals who cannot get away from themselves. Unless they accept help and are willing to follow the advice of others, they will successfully destroy themselves, if not through suicide then through living a life all distorted by selfish values and reasoning that is turned inward, distorted, out of focus, and off balance. In the process they will reach out, as it were, with unseen tentacles to ensnare family members and friends. Many husbands, wives, children, and friends are made to suffer by the actions of such as these.

Sometimes the victims themselves are unsuspecting, so successful is the suicidal individual at playing his or her game. Others are aware of the individual's motives but feel trapped, helpless to do anything about the situation. There are many so-called Christian marriages, for example, that are being held together by the thinnest of threads—the threat of "I'll kill myself if you leave me," and to prove his or her intent, the individual will make an attempt, perhaps through an overdose of sleeping pills with some tranquilizers thrown in. "Now," she thinks with satisfaction, "he'll know I mean business. He won't leave me."

Young people play the same sort of dangerous game. "I've threatened to take my life," they will write to the *Hollywood Free Paper,* "but I can't think of any painless way." It is true that every suicide attempt or even the merest mention of the idea is a plea for help. Granted that many such pleas are selfish in nature, still they are not to be regarded lightly. Threats turn into action. A passive declaration of "I wish I were dead" becomes an act. Selfish, childish, impulsive—whatever names are attached to the act, it is sad, unnecessary, and an affront to God, one's family, the community, and society in general. The philosopher Immanuel Kant was correct when he said that suicide is an insult to humanity.

Many letters reveal the verbalized threat that has become action that was unsuccessful. "When I was fifteen, I tried to kill myself because I thought I had nothing to live for." Contrary to many would-be suicides, however, this young person recognized that it was Satan who was trying to destroy her. This, we believe, has to be the explanation when Christians try suicide.

Paul Myers, popularly known as First Mate Bob, founder of the worldwide radio ministry known as Haven of Rest, himself a former alcoholic who more than once wished himself dead but who miraculously came up from the basement of suicide and alcoholism, used to say, "Try the Savior's side instead of suicide." This is a beautifully expressed sentiment, but it is also more than that. It is a profound truth—the answer to that person who wishes himself dead or who selfishly thinks in terms of suicide in order to gain attention and sympathy.

There may be those reading this who will take offense and resent the implication that an attempt to take one's own life is often selfishly motivated, but the facts cannot be denied, as proven by research from many sources. Such organizations as the National Institute of Mental Health, Contact Teleministries, the World Health Organization, Rescue, Inc., and other suicide prevention centers, and the findings of many other organizations, psychiatrists, psychologists, pastors, and individuals trained to analyze suicide and suicide threats reveal that these are people who are not living at peace with themselves and/or others. Many diverse factors enter in, but one thing is sure: The suicide-thinking person is distraught, whether by his or her own doing or as a result of emotional upheaval caused by others.

Many young people have difficulties with interpersonal relationships. It happens, of course, with adults as well. Stormy love affairs, a broken romance, feelings of being rejected and abandoned, loss of self-esteem, divorce and domestic difficulties, death of a loved one—despair and helplessness result from life's crises, and instead of turning to the Savior's side—even though some of these people are Christians—they react and turn to suicide.

It is known that scholastic anxiety will trigger the suicide crisis. In his study of suicide, Earl A. Grollman concluded that a terrifying concern of many students is their inability to compete successfully in school. Failure brings not only disappointment and disapproval from one's parents but also a shattering of one's own personal confidence. Those who know the suicide victim often use these words: "He pushed himself too hard"; "She worried over her grades"; "He felt his marks weren't as good as they should be." [4]

One student suffering from such feelings sent to the *Hollywood Free Paper* office a letter that unmistakably shows this terror even in the writer's scrawl, which fluctuates from normal writing to giant-sized scribbled words where she cries out, "PLEASE HELP!" She accurately describes herself as "a nervous wreck" and again her writing becomes odd-sized, as her frenzy shows through. She then tells of borrowing a boy's pocketknife at school, running out of the building, and "slowly but surely cutting my wrist, but a friend stopped me and got me home in time."

Another young writer concluded that if she could think like some of her friends do, perhaps she wouldn't be "so bugged with thoughts about killing myself." She adds, "They think about God and Jesus at least fifteen hours of the day. I wish I could get that 'high' on Him. Please tell me how. I need good advice."

Other heartbreaking letters reveal suicidal thoughts of young people "deep into sex orgies," "being strung out on drugs for years," and feelings of "going down the drain."

"I'd rather take my life than go on like this," one young man wrote. "I need courage to believe in myself and life without drugs. I'm twenty-nine years old now, but I'm still a child—a man, yet I act like a child. I want to love and live like a man—a Christian man." God stands ready to help such a person. Sometimes He'll help in very unusual ways. The writer of this same letter relates how God helped him one day.

> I really didn't think there was anything to Christianity. But now I'm beginning to see that Jesus has talked to me in many ways in the past, and He's still doing that. The other day I was out looking for drugs and was having no luck. I decided I'd ask God for help. I didn't feel it would work when I drove up behind a car, a car with a sign that read, "ONE WAY, ONE WAY WITH JESUS." Jesus was talking to me. I started looking around and saw a lot of cars with other messages similar to that so I started reading them and taking them as help from God in answer to my prayer. Was that right? So now I've started believing God is real and alive and life seems more worthwhile. I'm having trouble, however, living up to God's teachings. My old way of thinking gets in the way. I understand the world of drugs more than I understand the world of God. I can hide in drugs with friends who get as down as I am. I guess what I need is more faith—but it's sure hard. I'm having lots of trouble living the life Jesus wants me to live. When I get down, it's really a fight between the right and the wrong thing to do. I guess you could say I'm fighting the devil, right?
>
> When I give in to the devil though, it hurts me more than it used to. Is that good? Is God talking to me and telling me how to live and am I fighting Him? It's hard to do the right thing, but I haven't given up on what I know God can do for me. I just find it hard getting my life right with my selfish wants.

And that, dear reader, sums it up most accurately. It's what we've been trying to say in this entire chapter. What is it that drives a person into the elevator that takes him or her down to suicidal depression? Read once again that last statement from the young man which shows great insight—God-given insight, we feel certain—into the problem: "I just find it hard getting my life right with my *selfish wants*."

Anyone who acknowledges that stands in great company, with none other than the Apostle Paul himself. Paul, who cried out, "I can't help myself," as he portrayed the dilemma he found himself in, much like the young man who wrote this letter, said:

> I don't understand myself at all, for I really want to do what is right, but I can't. I do what I don't want to—what I hate. I know perfectly well that what I am doing is wrong, and my bad conscience proves that I agree with these laws I am breaking. But I can't help myself, because I'm no longer doing it. It is sin inside me that is stronger than I am that makes me do these evil things.
>
> I know I am rotten through and through so far as my old sinful nature is concerned. No matter which way I turn I can't make myself do right. I want to but I can't. When I want to do good, I don't; and when I try not to do wrong, I do it anyway. Now if I am doing what I don't want to, it is plain where the trouble is: sin still has me in its evil grasp.
>
> It seems to be a fact of life that when I want to do what is right, I inevitably do what is wrong. I love to do God's will so far as my new nature is concerned, but there is something else deep within me, in my lower nature, that is at war with my mind and wins the fight and makes me a slave to the sin that is still within me. In my mind I want to be God's willing servant but instead I find myself enslaved to sin.
>
> So you see how it is: my new life tells me to do right, but the old nature that is still inside me loves to sin. Oh, what a terrible predicament I'm in! Who will free me from my slavery to this deadly lower nature? Thank God! It has been done by Jesus Christ our Lord. He has set me free (Rom. 7:15–25).

Good-bye Empty
Endless Tomorrows!

Suicide is a fatal game that leads from
lucidity in the face of existence to a
flight from light.
Albert Camus

There is a land of the living and a land
of the dead and the bridge is love—
the only survival, the only meaning.
Wilder

"If you can really convince me of the existence of a supernatural,
all-powerful, busybody, know-it-all God, I promise to send you
my Satanic Bible." That was the conclusion of a long letter from
a sixteen-year-old who admitted to having tried suicide six
different times.

Someone else wrote:

> My old man hates me and my life is all messed up. I am
> fifteen and pretending in front of my old lady to be a new
> Christian. I don't know yet if Christ is the answer to the
> emptiness I feel. I've been into drinking, drugs, sex, robbing
> —everything. I've been thinking a lot about trying suicide
> next.

Another letter stated:

> A friend and I decided to end it all and so we went into a drug store and ripped off two boxes of car sickness pills. Life seemed so empty. Then we went into the bathroom of a service station, we could hardly walk and we saw horrible things all night long. We were half out of our minds and then my friend started screaming for me to call an ambulance. He just about died at the hospital and then started praying to God not to let him die. He accepted Jesus that night, and I did just recently.

The suicide has very ambivalent feelings. One moment he is certain that he wants to die; a short while later he is convinced that if he can just hold on a while longer, life is worth living. Sigmund Freud, the founder of psychoanalysis, authored the earliest psychological explanation of suicide, in which he shows this contradiction in life of self-preservation and self-destructiveness. There are basically two strong drives in one's life: the life instinct, or Eros; and the death, destructive, and aggressive drive, or Thanatos. Freud explained suicide as aggression turned upon the self, whereas murder is aggression turned upon another. Thus, suicide becomes murder in the 180th degree. Both suicide and murder are aspects of Thanatos.[1]

There are many who question whether or not the Bible makes some kind of precise statement about suicide. It does not, except to show the value of life and to make commands and state life principles. It is quite generally agreed among Christians that to kill one's self is incompatible with God's will for one's life. The commandment "Thou shalt not kill" is referred to, since the suicide, in making himself the object of murder, is still also its subject!

Throughout the Bible we are told that we do not belong to ourselves. We belong to God. "Behold, all souls are mine" (Ezek. 18:4, *AV*). "The Lord kills, The Lord gives life" (1 Sam. 2:6). It would appear that God is saying that when He gives us life, we are not to say yes to death by our own volition and will; He reserves to Himself the right of life *and* death.

The Apostle Paul must have been confronted frequently with Christians who wished to end it all. He built a very strong case to show that we do not belong to ourselves. He wrote to the Corinthian Christians in regard to all sorts of problems they were facing, many of which touched upon lust and easily recognized sinful practices. He summed it all up by stating, "Haven't you yet learned that your body is the home of the Holy Spirit God gave you, and that he lives within you? Your own body does not belong to you. For God has bought you with a great price, so use every part of your body to give glory back to God, because he owns it" (1 Cor. 6:19–20).

To the Roman Christians Paul wrote,

> Oh, what a wonderful God we have! How great are his wisdom and knowledge and riches! How impossible it is for us to understand his decisions and his methods! For who among us can know the mind of the Lord? Who knows enough to be his counselor and guide? And who could ever offer to the Lord enough to induce him to act? For everything comes from God alone. Everything lives by his power, and everything is for his glory. To him be glory forevermore.
>
> And so, dear brothers, I plead with you to give your bodies to God. Let them be a living sacrifice, holy—the kind he can accept. When you think of what he has done for you, is this too much to ask (Rom. 11:33–36; 12:1)?

So although the Bible does not give definite restrictions that precisely state "Don't kill yourself" or "Don't commit suicide," nowhere do we find the Lord approving of self-murder. God certainly does not sanction murder, and it is regarded as a vile sin. Therefore, in the face of all this, one must conclude that God is the giver and sustainer of life for anyone and everyone. There must come the recognition of the sovereignty of God and also that sometimes—oftentimes, in fact—God wills for us a fellowship of suffering. Even though life may appear to be a series of empty endless tomorrows, as a letter writer stated elsewhere in this chapter, we, as the Apostle Paul said, do not know enough to be God's counselor and guide. We are not calling the plays; God is in control. When we give ourselves to Him in faith, we give over the reins of our lives completely and respond in loving obedience, even though it may mean suffering and great difficulty.

Dr. Karl Menninger, who has delved deeply into the subject of suicide, contends that before a suicide can be consummated, there must exist the wish *to kill,* the wish *to be killed,* and the wish *to die.*[2] This, too, is incompatible with sound Christian thinking, for hatred is involved, and the Christian life is to be one of love —love for one's self, one's neighbor (family members and the like), and God. This is all biblical. The suicide is thinking and acting in a predominantly infantile way, for it is the way of a child to resent thwarting in any manner. Children are very possessive. They selfishly resent anything being taken away that they feel is their right to possess. In short, the child does not always respond in love.

One might excuse the child for lashing out vindictively, but in an adult, one who maintains normal intelligence but makes an unsuccessful suicide try, it is often difficult to respond with sympathy, especially where there is a history of words spoken and acts done to elicit sympathy, to make somebody worry about them, and to get attention. People such as these somehow need to be jolted out of their own self-centeredness. One writer says:

> If a man in despair cannot see his God, let him see the intolerable situation imposed upon wife or husband by the suicidal act, the damage to friends, the harm to which he often exposes others.
> Pity the parents and the children of a suicide case. The parents, always wondering if in some vital way they failed

their child. The children, who must go through life haunted by the thought that the same cruel seed of self-destruction sleeps in their subconscious, waiting to come awake. The stigma of suicide haunts the survivors for the remainder of their lives.[3]

Earlier in this chapter we stated that the suicide has ambivalent feelings. Things look hopeless, but at the same time there is a shred of hope to which he clings, hoping to be rescued. Dr. Karl Menninger points out, "Anyone who has sat by the bedside of a patient dying from a self-inflicted wound and listened to pleadings that the physician save his life, the destruction of which had only a few hours or minutes before been attempted, must be impressed by the paradox that one who has wished to kill himself does not wish to die!" [4]

Usually a suicidal episode occurs in the form of a crisis of limited duration. That is why it is so important for each of us to be "bridges of love" to those with whom we come in contact. You never know what your smile, your cheery "Hello, how are you?" and your kindness—even to a total stranger—may mean to that individual at that particular juncture in his life. Of particular importance, of course, is the need for family members to communicate love to one another in both big and little ways.

Suicide prevention centers and the organized efforts of society to decrease the number of suicides are doing much to communicate to the lonely, the disenchanted, the depressed, and the alienated. But in a very real way each of us can serve as a suicide prevention center by communicating love and understanding. On the whole, society is too busy, too indifferent, and really quite callous. We live, actually, quite an isolated existence, even in our more densely populated urban areas. This was strikingly shown—in a calamitous example of human isolation—in the suicide death of a college student found in his room after he had been dead eighteen days. What a tragic commentary on his existence! There were no friends, no one involved enough in his life to know or to care that he had been missing for more than two weeks.

Often we are simply unaware or unthinking in our dealings with those around us. But we, as Christians, have a tremendous responsibility to be conveyors of love. The letters we have been sharing in this book point up the fact that Satan is working overtime to destroy lives—especially those of young people, who are, it seems, especially vulnerable to his devious ways.

One wishes that all of the young people who write such desperate letters could have the insight that some of them display in their letters, like this one:

> I was a witch for quite awhile, but after reading the *Hollywood Free Paper* Jesus revealed Himself to me in all His real glory. I decided to follow His way but really didn't know how to go about it and started falling away. I had kept all my "tools" of witchcraft, feeling they were harmless and only a hobby. Yet they were what was holding me back, but I couldn't see this because I was still serving them partly in my heart.
>
> Another issue of your paper showed me the hold Satan and witchcraft had on me. I shook so hard I was almost unable physically to throw the "tools" out when I tried to. But along with the rest of the bad things in my life, it was *all* thrown out and the Lord saw to it that I got into a group of Christians who meet nearby. The fellowship of God's people and the power of the Holy Spirit and Jesus have really saved me.

Recognition of Satan's power and hold over one's life is a giant step that puts an individual on the path of living that gives peace and purpose rather than veering off going sideways. One young girl of twenty said,

> I praise the Lord all the time that He has rescued me. I get awfully lonely, but I don't want to go back into my old ways with old friends and the world's ways. Sometimes the devil

almost gets to me, but he's a liar and I have to remember that. Sometimes I'm a fool, however, and I do listen to him. I think the answer is to keep on trusting God, believing Jesus and praising Him!

She is correct. Paul says,

We are saved by trusting. And trusting means looking forward to getting something we don't yet have—for a man who already has something doesn't need to hope and trust that he will get it. But if we must keep trusting God for something that hasn't happened yet, it teaches us to wait patiently and confidently.

And in the same way—by our faith—the Holy Spirit helps us with our daily problems and in our praying. For we don't even know what we should pray for, nor how to pray as we should; but the Holy Spirit prays for us with such feeling that it cannot be expressed in words. And the Father who knows all hearts knows, of course, what the Spirit is saying as he pleads for us in harmony with God's own will. And we know that all that happens to us is working for our good if we love God and are fitting into his plans (Rom. 8:24–28).

Another letter, this one from a young married woman, points up the truth that it is only God's Holy Spirit and the love of Jesus that keeps us from going sideways.

I am 19, married four months, but all my life I've been a loner. I was made to be a loner until now. I had these ideals of truth and I came across too many who were opposites, so I departed from the world into my own. I'd walk at any given time and weather, with everything on my mind. I now know that it was only Jesus Who walked with me and stayed and kept me. Although I took Him down sordid ways, almost losing myself in thoughts of suicide that became for me a daily request, He was always there to pick up the pieces, trying to tell me that He loved me. I could not understand human love or even believe in its existence, therefore I wouldn't look at Jesus' love. But one day I walked into a church and picked up and read a Bible. The church was empty of humans, but I felt the presence of what had been there all along. I knew it was Jesus, and for the first time I didn't cry myself to sleep that night, but smiled at no one but His love and my knowledge of it. Now, as I write this, Jesus and I are one in thoughts and tears. Up until now my life was one of empty endless tomorrows filled with rooms with corners that were too small for even me to fit into. Now it's different; there's Jesus. Good-bye empty endless tomorrows!

11

Go to the Top for Help

> The final act of suicide is basically a resolution, a movement, perceived as the only possible one, out of a life situation felt to be unbearable by one of low sense of competence, with hope extinguished.
>
> *Maurice L. Farber,*
> The Theory of Suicide [1]

Jesus makes the difference. An anonymous article in *These Times* magazine, written by a successful high school science teacher who loved his work, who was continually receiving salary raises and was liked and respected by students and colleagues yet was plagued by thoughts of wanting to kill himself, has as its title "Go to the Top for Help." [2] The author admits that "Satan had me by the nose, leading me around, and I didn't even know it." Life became for him "a living hell," but "death scared me because I had no real idea what lay beyond life." He came to the conclusion that he wanted out of life regardless of whom he hurt and regardless of what lay beyond the other side of death.

The writer's judgment is that the mental anguish that induces suicidal thoughts becomes emotional illness. Mental pain, like physical pain, can become so unbearable that in desperation the person is driven to a remedy so drastic that he destroys all in trying to save part. In his anguish, one fateful night, he walked over to a window, stared out at the bright moon, and in a demanding voice shouted, "God, Jesus, or whoever You are! If You're really out there! If You're real and alive. If You can save me, You'd better do it in the next five minutes or forget about it!" He dropped to his knees and started to cry as he thought of the terrible things he'd done in his life and felt the urge to confess them, seeking forgiveness.

He describes what happened like this:

> An unknown, yet exhilarating, feeling settled over me, like I had been covered with a blanket of love. I cannot describe exactly how I felt, but perhaps the feeling can best be expressed in the words of a teenager who having just been converted ran up to me and shouted, "I've got God! I've got God!" That's somewhat like I felt, I had God, or maybe more correctly, He had me. After years and years of wandering, ignoring, guessing, doubting, and playing games, God was alive and real to me! I got up, weak from emotional exhaustion but strong with joy and hope, climbed back into bed and slept peacefully the rest of the night.

> The Bible says that faith comes from hearing and hearing from the word of God (Rom. 10:17). During the next few days God began to develop my faith in Him and reveal to me just what had happened on the night I almost took my life. He guided me to particular passages in the Scriptures. I had not read the Bible for a long, long time. I didn't know where to begin. All I knew was that I should begin. I thumbed through its pages at random. Providentially I stopped at Psalm 40 and read: "I waited patiently for God to help me; then he listened and heard my cry. He lifted me out of the pit of despair, out from the bog and the mire, and set my feet on a hard, firm path and steadied me as I walked along. He has given me a new song to sing" (Ps. 40:1–3).

I couldn't believe my eyes. The text told exactly what God had done for me—with one big exception. The man who wrote this psalm had waited patiently for God to help him. But not me! In my sin and pride I had demanded a reply from God right on the spot. Even so, God in His great love had listened. He had heard my cry for help. He had saved me. What a God! Again I flipped the pages, this time stopping at Psalm 139. My eyes fell on verse 7: "I can *never* be lost to your Spirit! I can *never* get away from my God! If I go up to heaven, you are there; if I go down to the place of the dead, you are there" (Ps. 139:7–8).

Once more God revealed to me through His Word the depth of His concern for me. A few days before I had almost taken my life, with Satan standing there ready to yank me into eternity with him, when the Lord intervened and pulled me back to safety. The fellow who wrote these words really knew what he was talking about. God is everywhere!

The author concludes the telling of his experience by stating, "I do not know exactly why God saved me from myself . . . but He did, and I'm mighty thankful. . . . Man-sized problems require God-sized solutions. Go to the top for help."

To those who write stating, "I am so sick of life sometimes I wonder what am I living for. I wish someone would kill me. I wish someone would put me in a cellar and throw away the key. I want to be happy and have something to live for. Can you help me?" our answer is exactly what the science teacher who wanted out of life prescribed: Go to the top for help.

Sylvia Plath, a brilliant young successful writer, wanted out of this life also. As one views the suicide scene, taking into account those who have taken their own lives, it comes as a shock to discover how many talented, brilliant, and successful people end up taking their own lives. It gives credence to a fact that Christianity has long expounded, that success in and of itself, and possessions, cannot and do not make a person happy. One could point, for example, to the late Marilyn Monroe and other well-known (in their time) artists, politicians, writers, and creative people who have despaired of living when they discovered a final nothingness that existed in their creative worlds. Self-destruction among highly creative people is not rare.

Alvarez, in his study on suicide, takes the reader through a journey where one views the act of suicide as the end of a long experience, an emptiness so isolated and violent as to make life into such a paper-thin reality of hopelessness that the individual finally surrenders. He describes the final suicide act of Sylvia Plath, who was his friend.[3]

Miss Plath herself wrote a fictionalized account of her struggle with herself and the events in her life, one of which was the time she went into the cellar of their home, crawled into the darkest, most inaccessible place she could find, carrying with her a tall glass of water and fifty sleeping pills that she'd taken from her mother's bureau drawer, and pushed "heavy, dust-covered logs across the hole mouth. The dark felt thick as velvet. I reached for the glass and the bottle, and carefully, on my knees, with bent head, crawled to the farthest wall. . . . I unscrewed the bottle of pills and started taking them swiftly, between gulps of water, one by one by one." [4] But that was not to be the end of Sylvia Plath. Some time later, she was discovered and miraculously survived that first suicide attempt.

When I read the letter from the young person stating he wished he could crawl into a cellar and die, I immediately thought of Sylvia Plath's experience—an experience that resulted in her spending a great amount of time in and out of hospitals and institutions where she was kept for psychotherapy and shock treatment. She described it as "A time of darkness, despair, disillusion—so black only as the inferno of the human mind can be—symbolic death, and numb shock—then the painful agony of slow rebirth and psychic regeneration." [5]

Later—much later—she was to end her own life successfully in a London flat by turning all the gas jets on and putting her head on the oven door. Alvarez believes this was a final desperate "cry for help" that fatally misfired. He believes that she expected to be found in time, but "her calculations went wrong and she lost." He says "her vision was blinkered by depression and illness." He feels "she was an enormously gifted poet whose death came carelessly, by mistake and too soon." [6]

In a world that is becoming increasingly superficial and artificial, when one does not go to the top for help or acknowledge that there is Someone at the top Who can give help and hope, then suicide seems far more desirable than does living a life of pretense in hopelessness. This was shown in the despair that preceded and prompted the death by suicide of two young people, seventeen-year-old versions of the all-American dream, as told in the book *Craig and Joan: Two Lives for Peace.*[7] It is the tragic but true story of two bright, popular students who died on October 15, 1969, their lives sucked out of their bodies by a vacuum cleaner hose attached to the car exhaust. It is a distressing story of pain, love, and terror, but the book dramatically points up the high ideals and the dreams and hopes of young people today living in a society that is becoming increasingly complex.

Craig and Joan were not drug addicts or morally depraved individuals. They did everything in the power of a teen-aged cheerleader and a teen-aged intelligent young fellow to convince those they knew and loved of the importance of right living. They were both deeply concerned about war. Death seemed to be the best way to have an impact on people's thinking, to be convincing. They left behind twenty-four notes of explanation and desire, but only two of them were ever printed.

What Craig and Joan apparently failed to realize is that they did not have to make that kind of sacrifice—their own lives—that Someone had preceded them in sacrificing His life. As Jesus said of Himself while talking to the disciples one time when they were disputing who would be the greatest among them, "I, the Messiah, did not come to be served, but to serve, and to give my life as a ransom for many" (Matt. 20:28).

Paul the Apostle described the giving of Jesus' life like this: "There is only one God, and only one intermediary between God and men, Jesus Christ the man. He gave himself as a ransom for us all—an act of redemption which happened once, but which stands for all time as a witness to what he is" (1 Tim. 2:5–6).[8]

Paul said that, incredible as it may sound, this is what actually happened and accepting this, believing it, and acting on what Jesus has done puts a man moving in the direction of being saved from himself and the evil in this world that surrounds him constantly. We live in a world where there will be constant strife, war, and an absence of peace. Taking one's own life in protest for the inequities of life isn't going to alter the situation. It may produce a disturbing and unsettling effect on those closest to the one or ones who may do as Craig and Joan did, and it may even have a rippling effect on others, but the long-range effect is not worthy of such a terrible and senseless sacrifice of life.

Christ came into this world that we might have life and that we might have it more abundantly. He explained this so beautifully in the parable of the Good Shepherd, where He speaks of sheep recognizing the voice and following the Shepherd and of the thief coming into the sheepfold with the purpose of stealing, killing, and destroying. Jesus said:

> My purpose is to give life in all its fullness. I am the Good Shepherd. The Good Shepherd lays down his life for the sheep. . . . The Father loves me because I lay down my life that I may have it back again. No one can kill me without my consent—I lay down my life voluntarily. For I have the right and power to lay it down when I want to and also the right and power to take it again. For the Father has given me this right (John 10:10b, 11, 17, 18).

Jesus was stating that there can be ecstasy in living—the kind of ecstasy Craig and Joan were seeking and wanted for themselves and others. Idealistic young people, but adults too, need to see this and be challenged to grasp both the good and the bad of life and allow God to use it.

We are actually very much like lost wandering sheep. Jesus' illustration, as with all His parables, so perfectly fitted the need to which He was addressing Himself. In lonely desperation, there are those who wander aimlessly, shepherdless. Such as these are easy prey for that thief of thieves, Satan himself, who would snatch them away into death. No wonder David the psalmist said:

> The Lord is my shepherd; I shall not want. He maketh me to lie down in green pastures; he leadeth me beside the still waters. He restoreth my soul: he leadeth me in the paths of righteousness for his name's sake. Yea, though I walk through the valley of the shadow of death, I will fear no evil: for thou art with me; thy rod and thy staff they comfort me. Thou preparest a table before me in the presence of mine enemies: thou anointest my head with oil; my cup runneth over. Surely goodness and mercy shall follow me all the days of my life: and I will dwell in the house of the Lord forever (Ps. 23, *AV*).

Because David knew God as a Shepherd, he was conscious of God's leading, even through valleys—the valley of the shadow of death itself—and with God guarding, guiding, providing, protecting, David knew that whatever happened was God's will. Even though it might appear unbelievably agonizing, terribly traumatic, all wrong and senseless, still God was in it, and David could speak of God's goodness and unfailing kindness. That kind of trusting and believing will take a person through the darkest of valleys.

12

Suicide and Good Mental Health

But to be spiritually minded is
life and peace.
Rom. 8:6b, AV.

What a man thinketh in his heart,
he advertises on his face.
Reader's Digest

The letter was signed "Down and Out," which pretty accurately describes the condition of that one caught on the elevator down into depression. How easy it is once one has slid into depression to slide away from faith and into the abyss of suicide. Those in the know—whose business it is to deal with suicides—say that the surest preventive is to make certain that a person keeps his mental health and bounce. The Reverend Lloyd Workman, director of the Help Line Contact Clinic of Greater Los Angeles, states that a key word from anyone dealing with a would-be suicide (both from a theological or a psychological side) is acceptance.

There are many who wonder just what good mental health is. Another letter writer says:

> I have a very unorthodox question, but perhaps you have been confronted with it before. If drug addicts can be cured by accepting Christ into their lives, etc., why doesn't the same procedure work for the emotionally or mentally disturbed? How can a real Christian find himself in such straits? I am such an individual and I've considered myself a Christian for many years. I can hardly believe what is happening to me and I'm afraid I'm due for a hospital unless something intervenes. I've tried many things to no avail.

This letter was from a Bible-believing Christian, one who regularly attends a home Bible-study class.

Russell Palmer, in his pamphlet *The Lengthening Shadow of Suicide,* suggests that one should recognize that mental health is something positive and not the mere absence of mental illness. Here is the simple checklist he recommends to gauge whether or not you are in good mental health:

1. Mental health is being in balance, as God made you, not tossed around by your emotions.
2. Mental health is being comfortable with yourself, as well as with other people.
3. Mental health is finding satisfaction in the things that occupy your time, both work and play.
4. Mental health is doing something about your responsibilities and your problems.[1]

Mr. Palmer refers to the National Association for Mental Health and some constructive steps drawn up by Dr. George S. Stevenson to help safeguard one's mental health:

1. TALK IT OUT. Don't bottle it up. Confide your worry to some level-headed person you can trust.
2. ESCAPE FOR A WHILE. Of course a change helps,

whether it is a change of activity, scene, or people. Lets you recover breath and balance.

3. WORK OFF YOUR ANGER. Let your "revenge" wait until tomorrow. Meanwhile work off your pent-up energy by doing something.

4. GIVE IN OCCASIONALLY. Giving in once in a while —even if you are dead right—is easy on your system. When you give in, others will too!

5. DO SOMETHING FOR OTHERS. Doing something for somebody else is a wonderful way to stop worrying about yourself. Make it something positive and helpful—and perhaps unexpected!

6. TAKE ONE THING AT A TIME. Are you over-worked? You can clear it up, more easily and quickly than you believe, by tackling just one thing at a time.

7. GO EASY ON YOURSELF. Don't expect too much of yourself. No one can be perfect in everything.

8. GO EASY WITH YOUR CRITICISM. Don't expect too much of others. Instead of being critical, search out the other fellow's good points and help him to develop them.

9. GIVE THE OTHER FELLOW A BREAK. No need to "get there first" or to edge the other fellow out. Go easy. If he feels that you are no longer a threat to him, he will stop being a threat to you.

10. MAKE YOURSELF AVAILABLE. Feel rejected? Don't withdraw and sulk. Chances are that people are waiting for you to make the first move.

11. SCHEDULE YOUR RECREATION. Don't drive your-self. Let up and relax—*frequently*.[2]

What could be listed as suggestion number twelve or what one might have used to head up the list or, better still, what could be written across the entire list and what Dr. Stevenson points out as basic to good mental health is FAITH. He defines it, as it has been defined frequently throughout this volume, as faith in God, in yourself, and in others.[3]

The best way to obtain such faith is to come to God in all

honesty, with all of life's raw edges exposed (He sees them and knows all about them anyway), voicing your feelings, doubts, or whatever is in your heart and on your mind. The Bible gives assurance that God will never ignore a broken, humble heart. We ourselves have used Psalm 51 to clear up our relationship with Him. David wrote this Psalm after he had grievously sinned against God and Bathsheba's husband, Uriah.

O loving and kind God, have mercy. Have pity upon me and take away the awful stain of my transgressions. Oh, wash me, cleanse me from this guilt. Let me be pure again. For I admit my shameful deed—it haunts me day and night. It is against you and you alone I sinned, and did this terrible thing. You saw it all, and your sentence against me is just. But I was born a sinner, yes, from the moment my mother conceived me. You deserve honesty from the heart; yes, utter sincerity and truthfulness. Oh give me this wisdom.

Sprinkle me with the cleansing blood and I shall be clean again. Wash me and I shall be whiter than snow. And after you have punished me, give me back my joy again. Don't keep looking at my sins—erase them from your sight. Create in me a new, clean heart, O God, filled with clean thoughts and rightful desires. Don't toss me aside, banished forever from your presence. Don't take your Holy Spirit from me. Restore to me again the joy of your salvation, and make me willing to obey you. Then I will teach your ways to other sinners, and they—guilty like me—will repent and return to you. Don't sentence me to death, O my God, you alone can rescue me. Then I will sing of your forgiveness, for my lips will be unsealed—oh, how I will praise you.

You don't want penance; if you did, how gladly would I do it! You aren't interested in offerings burned before you on the altar. It is a broken spirit you want—remorse and penitence. A broken and contrite heart, O God, you will not ignore (Ps. 51:1–17).

The science teacher who had contemplated suicide (mentioned in the previous chapter) offers four suggestions to the severely depressed person. First, don't think that you can work, play, drink, smoke, take drugs, ignore, read, study, talk, or forget your way out of your dilemma. You can't. If you could solve your problems on your own, you wouldn't be in the mess you're in. He suggests that you transfer your burdens of sin and guilt to God and that confession will have a cleansing, uplifting effect on you.

Second, if you want to be permanently cured of your depression, you must go a step beyond confession and ask Jesus Christ to come into your life on a personal and permanent basis as your Lord and Savior. Only as you continually cling to Him for strength and guidance will you find victory over the destructive forces within you. Third, focus your thoughts and actions on the good and positive in life. Brooding about the negative inevitably brings depression. Again, Christ's power working in and through you will enable you to focus on the good and positive. Fourth, seek out the friendship of mature Christians—people experiencing daily victory over sins in their lives through continual contact with Jesus Christ. If you don't know anyone like that, ask God to help you find him. He will.[4]

Poor mental health is not always easily recognizable in others and sometimes even in one's self. You may be restless, dissatisfied, or unhappy without realizing that you are actually in a flat mood of deep depression. Depression is a word we shy away from; we don't like it in others and don't like to admit we may be depressing to be around. Depression in young people may not show itself in the same way it does in adults. Parents may mistake defiance, wild behavior, tantrums, even fatigue in their children as something other than what it actually is —depression. It has been shown in a study of adolescent suicides that almost all of the victims' mothers were depressed individuals preoccupied with suicidal thoughts. It is distressingly true that the majority of suicides have suffered from depression.

Mental illness as such, however, is not easily defined, and many who are mentally ill are not necessarily psychotic—that is, the great majority of suicides are in touch with reality; although they may be desperate, they are not candidates for a mental hospital. Actually, less than one-quarter of suicidal patients are psychotic. The rate of suicide among schizophrenics and manic-depressives, however, is high.

A great profusion of material has been amassed dealing with suicidal behavior. There is a wealth of social, psychiatric, and psychological information. This book is only skimming the surface, and readers are strongly advised to investigate further for more precise information. The U.S. Public Health Service has an up-to-date bibliography showing the contributions that have been made in such findings and literature. Local suicide prevention centers, the National Institute of Mental Health, local libraries, and books that can be found in bookstores will contribute vast amounts of material for anyone who wishes to pursue the study of suicidal behavior and its prevention in more detail.

From the accumulated mass of information it can be definitely stated that distress, despair, unhappiness, poor interpersonal relationships, social disorganization, and adverse early (childhood) experiences are all notable features of attempted or completed suicides. Self-destruction is not a theological issue; Grollman says and we agree, it is the result of unbearable emotional stress.[5] There are all sorts of variables and precipitating factors, but those who attempt suicide are people whose lives are most frequently characterized by social and psychological deficits that pose severe problems for them, their family members, and those who attempt to help and treat them. The suicidal person is suffering from what has been described as "tunnel vision"—that is, a limited focus, with his mind unable to furnish him with a complete picture of how to handle his seemingly intolerable problems.

For the young woman who questioned how a Christian could possibly find herself in an emotional or mentally disturbed state, the answer is that we cannot violate natural and spiritual laws and expect to get away with it without suffering some adverse effect. Despondency, depression, emotional and mental upheaval are great weapons of our astute adversary, the devil. The depths of despondency were known by some of the most outstandingly successful prophets in Scripture. Their depression was rooted in deep-seated causes, some of which have already been shown in Chapter 1. We have briefly referred there to Moses, Elijah, and Jonah, each of whom expressed the desire that God would take life away from him.

God did not honor their foolish requests, but had His own certain remedy for each. Dr. J. Oswald Sanders, in his book *A Spiritual Clinic,* believes there was a threefold background to the despondency of each of these men: (1) *physiological* —their physical endurance was overtaxed, they were under great emotional stress and strain, and there was both mental and physical exhaustion; (2) *selfishness*—they engaged in an orgy of self-pity becoming self-engrossed; there was a resentment of God's grace and forbearance when they felt their own reputations had been put on the spot—they had prophesied judgment and God had exercised mercy; in each case the desire to die stemmed from making self and self-interest supreme instead of God and His glory (Sanders asks, "Is not all despondency in essence a manifestation of self in one form or another?"); and (3) *spiritual* —spiritual disappointment and a sense of failure, a feeling of being out of touch with God, existed.[6]

Sanders draws up these lessons for us today from the episodes in the lives of these men:

1. Overexpenditure of physical and nervous capital, even in desperately needy areas of the Lord's service, gives the adversary opportunity to attack our spirits. We overspend at our peril.
2. Despondency can follow spiritual success as easily as spiritual failure.
3. We must seek physical and spiritual renewal if we are not to be put to flight by our enemy.

4. If we shift our center from God to self, even for a period, we lay ourselves open to this malady of the spirit.
5. We should give weight to the advice of our Jethros. (Jethro was Moses' father-in-law, who advised him to get additional help in his administration of the Israelites.) Delegation of work and dropping of some commitments can bring a speedy resurgence of spiritual optimism.
6. Physical precautions can prevent sunstroke or malaria, not to mention neurasthenia and heart afflictions. (Jonah, you will recall, suffered what is believed by many to have amounted to good old-fashioned sunstroke.)
7. Discouragement over the apparent failure of our best efforts, if not met with the shield of faith, will react disastrously on our spirits and degenerate into self-pity and despair. Such failure is sometimes more apparent than real—as with Elijah and the 7,000.
8. Going to bed early and a change of diet will settle many a case of depression. "I have so much to do," said the French philosopher Le Maistre, "that I must go to bed."
9. God prescribes individually for each of His patients.
10. God delights to restore each depressed soul to a sphere of increased usefulness.[7]

"Above all, taking the shield of faith, wherewith ye shall be able to quench all the fiery darts of the wicked" (Eph. 6:16, *AV*). You cannot read the Bible without recognizing that God's servants did go through great trials. They experienced domestic tragedy, as in the case of the prophet Hosea. These men of God did not find answers to their complex problems in tranquilizers and stimulants but in conforming to the will of God as they earnestly sought for this. This is not to minimize the help of modern medical means and the role of those trained to help (as emphasized elsewhere), but it is an honest recognition that most physical and mental illnesses are the manifestation of inner resentments, tensions, and fears. We can help ourselves immensely while going through such turmoil by minding our minds.

Just how does one mind his mind? By claiming God's promise, "Thou wilt keep him in perfect peace, whose mind is stayed on thee" (Isa. 26:3, *AV*). The mind has been likened to the control tower at an airport, where someone in authority is governing the actions of the planes for landing and takeoff. Just so, our minds control our lives; and if our minds are stayed on God, He will control our lives. If we want spiritual and emotional health, then our minds must be ruled by the Holy Spirit.

The Bible tells us how to control our thought life. You can find many references that prove that "As a man thinketh in his heart, so is he" (Prov. 23:7, *AV*). *Reader's Digest* once stated, "What a man thinketh in his heart, he advertises on his face." The following are just a few biblical references concerning the thought life: 2 Cor. 10:5; Rom. 12:3; Phil. 2:5; Prov. 4:23; Matt. 12:34; Ps. 139:2; and there are hundreds of others. The pattern for control of your thought life is given in Philippians: "Fix your thoughts on what is true and good and right. Think about things that are pure and lovely, and dwell on the fine, good things in others. Think about all you can praise God for and be glad about" (Phil. 4:8). The preceding verse in Philippians promises God's peace, described as being far more wonderful than the human mind can understand, when we allow Him to keep our thoughts and hearts quiet and at rest as we trust Christ Jesus (Phil. 4:7).

It has been pointed out that in giving the beatitudes, when Christ said, "Blessed are the pure in heart: for they shall see God" (Matt. 5:8, *AV*), He did not say pure in actions or even pure in body, but pure in heart—going down to the depths of the thought life.

If there are those reading this who are struggling with their thought life, the way out of the dilemma is to do as Romans says: "And be not conformed to this world: but be ye transformed by the *renewing of your mind,* that ye may prove what is that good, and acceptable, and perfect, will of God" (Rom. 12:2, *AV*). Ephesians says the same thing: "And be *renewed in the spirit of your mind*" (Eph. 4:23, *AV*). [Authors' italics]

The reader is well advised to delve further into this by reading such things as the book *My Pursuit of Peace* by Dorothy Harrison Pentecost and *Why Christians Crack Up* by Marion H. Nelson, M.D., a seminary-trained Christian psychiatrist.[8] Your Christian bookstores can make other valuable suggestions. (See also the Acknowledgments at the front of this book.)

True spiritual strength comes as we depend on the Lord, and also as we learn to live within our own physical and mental limitations. This is not always so easy to learn or to accept. The reason many do not find the peace they long for is because they seek it on their own terms. They are unwilling to be renewed in the spirit of their minds, to change their ways of life and their ways of thinking. They just want peace added, period. We are first in our lives, and God second. Christ has told us unmistakably that only in Him can we have peace. "I have told you all this so that you will have peace of heart and mind. Here on earth you will have many trials and sorrows; but cheer up, for I have overcome the world" (John 16:33).

Peace has nothing to do with geography, circumstances, possessions, plans, and methods; nor can you obtain it through reading books of psychology or psychiatry. If you are "down and out," straining for what you feel should be good mental health, we suggest to you that you look into the Bible. There you will find the God-given prescription for peace, which can be received from Him in response to the conditions laid down by Him through His Word.

13

Faith, Hope, and Love

> Hope thou in God.
> *Ps. 42:5, AV*

I've tried suicide with pills and it didn't work, but no one knows. Nothing says I won't try again.

One night I took fifteen aspirin to kill myself, but it didn't work; I think about it all the time and that I should try again. Once Jesus helped me right before I opened up the bottle. But I think about doing it all the time.

I'm sixteen years old and an acid freak. I've read some of your stuff and I think you know where your head is at about your Jesus thing; you seem to be coming through. But I don't think I can accept Jesus because I love doing dope too much. But I wish these brothers of mine could be helped—we'll all be dead from the use of "H" within a year unless we stop. I wish you could help these dudes. Don't

bother with me. I don't want to stop doping or drinking.
I dig it too much. But still, I'd like to hear from you.

I don't know how to start this letter, so I'll start with a
confession—I'M DRUNK! I've sinned exceedingly in the
past, but I want to be saved. I guess I don't have the
strength however. I NEED YOUR PEACE. . . . PLEASE
HELP ME! I have to have alcohol to keep me down. . . .
I am plagued by Satan. [The letter rambled on with the
scrawl of a desperate drunk crying out, "I'm lost!"]

Four different letters representing four different individuals an-
guishing in their own private hell, each a cry for help, poignant
and dramatic, heartbreaking and real. Two had tried suicide, the
other two were committing what is called slow suicide by their
life-shortening activities; they are what is labeled either a partial,
subintentioned, submeditated suicide or a suicide equivalent. They
are hovering on the brink of self-destruction. One might call it
installment-plan suicide—less obvious perhaps, but deadly.

I wonder how many people reading this book are aware that
death by suicide takes a greater toll of life than do the combined deaths from typhoid fever, dysentery, scarlet fever, diph-
theria, whooping cough, meningococcal infections, infantile paral-
ysis, measles, typhus, malaria, bronchitis, and rheumatic fever,
according to Grollman's study of suicide.[1] Suicide, which once
ranked twenty-second on the list of causes of death in the United
States, now rates tenth, and in some states it is sixth. Thus, the
reason for the writing of this book. We send it out as a warning
signal. "A cry for help is a summons for rescue," states Justice
Benjamin Cardozo. We agree.

There is a fallacy abroad that needs to be laid to rest—the idea
that people who talk about suicide won't actually do it. Any
verbalized threat should be regarded seriously. There is yet another myth that exists that is likewise dangerously false—the
thought that once a person has attempted suicide and failed, he
won't do it again. "Twelve percent of those who attempt suicide

will make a second try and succeed within two years. Four out of five persons who do kill themselves have attempted to do so at least one time previously. After an abortive try, many resolve: 'I'll do a better job the next time.' And they mean it." [2]

The young girl who wrote saying, "Nothing says I won't try again," was not making an idle threat. She, like so many others, finds the world a lonely place—big, overly populated, lonely. People all around, but still someone will say, "I've never been so unhappy in my life. There's just *no one* to talk to." Breakdown in communication among family members and no or poor communication with friends or between husbands and wives or lovers is a contributing cause to the isolation the suicide feels that propels him into the act. Death is a relief from his psychic pain.

Dr. Thaddeus Kostrubala, formerly Chicago's mental health director, has commented that the public attitude toward suicide is weak, sinful, and a disgrace. Of those who succeed in killing themselves 85 percent have sought help in one way or another.[3]

Dr. Stanley F. Yolles, director of the National Institute of Mental Health, at one time said that 75 percent of all people who kill themselves go to a physician within a few months or weeks prior to their deaths, and often their suicidal symptoms remain undetected. "In over half the suicide deaths, there is a history of previous, spontaneous, suicidal communications, either direct— 'I'm going to shoot myself'—or indirect—'How do you leave your body to the medical school?' " Not only physicians but all of us must somehow learn to recognize more suicidal signals and know how to respond to them.[4] This holds particularly true among family members.

We have become a grimly depersonalized world, as evidenced by the many letters received at the *Hollywood Free Paper* office and by the statistics that tell the story of suicide. One letter on bright orange stationery (as if the writer was using what he felt could not go unnoticed or be bypassed) screamed out in its salutation, "PEOPLE!" The letter related a heartbreaking story of drug addiction, of being put into a rehabilitation center where things were, in the writer's words, "worse than hell and I tried to kill myself. After that, they let me leave." He pleads for help, stating that if he doesn't get it, they will find him dead.

The world is hostile to many insecure people who cannot cope and only wish escape. If they cannot bring themselves actually to commit suicide, they will live on the thin edge of death because of their daily intake of drugs, including alcohol. It has been found that barbiturate addicts purchase and store sleeping pills by the hundreds and take them day and night so that they get to the place where they cannot tolerate even a day without drugs. Such addicts frequently place themselves in a rather deep stage of anesthesia almost every night, according to investigators from the Los Angeles Suicide Prevention Center.

An article appeared in *Look* magazine [5] stating that some psychiatrists believe that most suicidal persons suffer from what is called manic-depressive disease, depressed phase. Instead of showing standard textbook symptoms of alternating periods of jubilation and dark despair, the patient sinks into a bleak morass of silent symptoms that may last many months. Appetite may diminish; the person loses weight, wakens at 4 A.M., and can't get back to sleep; he loses interest in sex and, perhaps, in his work and hobbies. If he sees a doctor, he will complain of vague, hypochondriacal symptoms but keep silent regarding his feelings of deep sadness, worthlessness, and unhappiness. This kind of depressed person is also usually overwhelmed with guilt and will frequently make such remarks as "I wish I were dead" or "I think that I'm really too much of a burden on you." These are all danger signals, and to be aware of them is to join the ranks of those who can rightly be called gatekeepers—those who are interested in *people* and willing and anxious to extend love and help.

Dr. Karl Menninger has stated that to the normal person suicide seems too dreadful and senseless to be conceivable. There almost seems to be a taboo on the serious discussion of it. There has never been a wide campaign against it, as there has been against less easily preventable forms of death. There is no organized public interest in it. Dr. Menninger believes that if the general population were made more aware of clues to suicidal danger, many suicides would be prevented. We cannot ignore natural death, but neither must we turn our backs on self-imposed death. According to Grollman,

> Suicide has been known in all times and committed by all manner of people, from Saul, Sappho, and Seneca to Virginia Woolf, James Forrestal, and Marilyn Monroe. Attempted self-destruction, whether completed or not, involves emotional turmoil, social discord, and terrifying disruption of life. No task demands so much skill, understanding, empathy, and support as ministering to those downcast people who can no longer find purpose in life, or to the family who has experienced the loss of a loved one through self-inflicted death.[6]

Reader's Digest had a special reprint feature entitled "The Awesome Power of Human Love" that focused on what is called the single most important force in shaping our physical, emotional, and spiritual lives.[7] Of course, it's not a new idea; we've all known it and heard it—great literature espouses the idea, music plays up the theme, and supremely the Bible emphasizes the need for and the power of love. But when one reads in the paper of a fifteen-year-old in London killing herself and leaving behind a note that says, "I'm just a dreamer and none of my dreams will ever come true. I just can't face reality. I wish someone would really love me," then the truth comes home with devastating impact.

An 1897 book by the noted suicide researcher Emile Durkheim gives some insight into the reasoning that leads many to kill themselves. Durkheim wrote, "Every suicide has an unsolvable and unsharable problem in the mind." This certainly points up the need for each of us to be conveyors of love, confirming the *Reader's Digest* feature showing the awesome power of human love.

A prison suicide had underscored heavily in his Bible a passage found in the fourth chapter of Ecclesiastes: "Two are better than one; because they have a good reward for their labour. For if they fall, the one will lift up his fellow: but woe to him that is alone when he falleth; for he hath not another to help him up" (Eccl. 4:9, *AV*).

A random sampling of newspaper headlines that we have gathered shows quite graphically what happens when someone "falls" and there is no one to lift him up:

HOPELESS LIVES SWELL THE SUICIDE ROLLS

DREAMS FAIL, DANCER CHOOSES DEATH AT 15

WOMAN DANGLES BY FOOT IN SUICIDE TRY

PRISONER FOUND HANGING IN CELL

7 YEARS A POW, DEAD AT 32—AF CAPTAIN LISTED AS SUICIDE

BOY'S PARENTS BAFFLED, TEENAGER CARRIES REASON
FOR HIS SUICIDE TO THE GRAVE

BLUE MONDAYS GO TO SUICIDAL EXTREME

AFTERMATH OF A PRISON SUICIDE

LEADERS UNDER STRESS—DEPRESSION CAN AFFECT THEIR ACTS

TO COP OUT OR TO COPE?

ANATOMY OF A TRAGEDY

THE YOUTHFUL SUICIDES

ORANGE COUNTY SUICIDE RATE CLIMB OUTSTRIPS POPULATION

GOLDEN GATE BRIDGE CLAIMS 501ST SUICIDE

CONFERENCE FOCUSES ON RISING SUICIDE RATE OF YOUNG BLACKS

HIGH SUICIDE RATES OF ESKIMOS STUDIED

STRAIN OF "LIBERATION" DRIVES MORE WOMEN TO SUICIDE

SUICIDE, A NEW ATTACK AGAINST AN OLD KILLER

1,000 SUICIDES A DAY REPORTED BY WORLD HEALTH ORGANIZATION

IN THE SPRING A YOUNG MAN'S FANCY OFTEN TURNS TO SUICIDE

The article under the latter headline emphasized that when spring comes, the suicide rate goes up. Life comes back to the earth ever so gently, and then often in a flood, and folks do themselves in in greater numbers than at any other time of the year. In spring, as the old saying goes, a young man's fancy lightly turns to thoughts of love. The world is luscious. Crocuses come, and daffodils—and death.

It may come as a surprise to many that holiday times are also times of increased suicides. The explanation probably is that people without families or close friendship ties feel the loneliness more then. People are not achieving the joy they normally associate and come to expect with the happiest of all seasons, and so at Christmas time, as well as early spring, more suicides occur than at any other time of year.

One psychiatrist has actually analyzed how some of his patients identified with the baby Jesus and how the Savior died that the faithful might live, so Christmas becomes part of a holiday syndrome. People in a distraught state of mind, desiring a new birth, a new chance, and wanting to get out of the entanglements and unsettled problems of this life, seek escape in death.

Yet, except for the holiday season, winter does not produce as many suicides as do other times of the year. It is not the bleak cold months, but spring, as stated before, when life is being renewed, when people do not feel up to starting the old cycle again, even though they have managed to survive the winter period, and when they cannot meet the challenge of rebirth and the renewal of life that are associated with spring; it is then that severe depression often increases and there is a rise in the number of suicides and requests for help.

The Bible records five suicides. Immediately there comes to mind the suicide of Judas, who betrayed Christ. The Word faithfully records that

> When he [Judas] saw that Jesus had been condemned to die, [he] changed his mind and deeply regretted what he had done, and brought back the money [paid to him to betray Jesus] to the chief priests and other Jewish leaders.
> "I have sinned," he declared, "for I have betrayed an innocent man."
> "That's your problem," they retorted.
> Then he threw the money onto the floor of the Temple and went out and hanged himself (Matt. 27:3–5).

Observe how Judas changed his mind, repented of what he had done, despaired, and was ruined—unlike Peter, another of Jesus' disciples who betrayed Jesus by denying Him. Peter repented, believed, sought pardon, and received it. Judas confessed that he had betrayed innocent blood, but there are those who believe he did not confess to salvation. Judas abandoned himself alone to despair and became his own executioner. Judas recognized that he had sinned, but there is no record that he appealed to the mercy of God in Christ. It is one thing to despair of helping ourselves, but we must never despair of the help of God. To destroy one's own life to ease one's conscience is not the answer.

A young girl wrote a letter of thanks to a woman who had helped her through a very traumatic time in her life. She, too, like Judas, had despaired and attempted to take her own life. The woman in whom she confided was able to help her build some fences around her problem so that she could trust somebody and not let the problem crush her. Later, a much happier young coed, she wrote the woman stating, "Thanks for holding on when I was letting go."

That's what salvation is all about. Is life heaping more on you than you think you can stand? Are you tired of stumbling over the debris of broken dreams and unfulfilled plans? Life is often a long, grim race. But you don't have to run it alone. Jesus is always there, ready to forgive our sins, remove our guilt, and hold on to us when we are tempted to let go.

If you were hanging by your fingernails to the edge of a cliff, close to losing your last hold on your mortal life, and someone came along who could grab your hand and rescue you from almost certain death, you'd let him hold on to you and save your life, wouldn't you? That is the picture of what God through Christ has done. In our sinful, lost state, God reached out, because He cared, because He loved us, and took our hands.

The Bible says that we are all facing an impending danger—the danger of eternal separation from everything that is good and worthwhile. Sin, anything opposite of what God wants, pulls us over the edge of the spiritual cliff. Our grip may be strong enough to hang on for a short time but not strong enough to pull ourselves up to safety. God knows that we are all strung out on the very brink of disaster; in fact, He sent His Son Jesus (even His Name means Savior) to provide us a way to be rescued from a fate that is literally worse than death—eternal separation from Him. God doesn't make us take Jesus' hand, however, but He does provide the means for escape.

If some of you reading this are hanging onto life by your finger-nails, as it were, on this brink of disaster, thinking perhaps of suicide as an escape and the way out, and you choose not to accept God's salvation and grasp onto the Reality of Jesus, then you will be committing eternal suicide. But if you will just place yourself into the Savior's hands, He will never let you go; He will save you. Jesus will tell you where to place your feet. He will endow you with inner resources capable of meeting every need and confronting every situation.

If it is true that the death of love evokes the love of death, then accept the fact that Jesus loves you with a love that far surpasses any earthly love of any human being and that in His love you can live and face the rest of today and the tomorrows. With this new identity in Christ you will gain security. You will "belong" to the family of God, and you will be loved. "I, I am He who comforts you; who are you that you should fear mortal man" (Isa. 51:12)?

Psychiatrist Victor Frankl has said, "Until a man has found meaning in death, he cannot hope to find meaning in life." There can be no meaningful death unless we are God's through Christ, and there can be no meaning in life so long as a man is not in Christ.

What then is the answer to living and dying? It is not *people,* but it is the power and help that come from God. It has been proven, as stated earlier in this book, that hope moves a person out of suicidal preoccupation. We recognize, however, that hope must be based on reality factors. Let there be the recognition then that life is not all beauty and joy. God's comfort and love is not a luxurious davenport, breakfast in bed, air-conditioning, a new car, or other external extras that may make living a little more enjoyable but not necessarily provide internal comfort.

God's comfort can make you strong in weakness. He may not take away your problems and He may not remove the Cross, but He will give you strength to bear it. He may not remove you from the battle, but He will give peace in the midst of personal war. He does not always remove adversity, but He gives courage to endure. Darkness and light, joy and sorrow, success and suffering—all of these are indispensable strands in the texture of existence.[8] But in and through it all, here is the ultimate answer: "Hope thou in God" (Ps. 42:5, *AV*).

"Why art thou cast down, O my soul?" the psalmist asked. And we ask it too. "Why art thou disquieted in me? Why downcast? Why be discouraged and sad? Why be depressed and gloomy? Trust in God! Praise Him for His wondrous help; He will make you smile again" (our paraphrase of Ps. 42:5; 43:5). Yes, we strongly recommend this: *"Hope thou in God."*

Note: If you would like to receive a free copy of the *Hollywood Free Paper,* write to Duane Pederson, Jesus People, Box 2131, Santa Monica, California 90406.

Appendix
Suicide Prevention Centers

Directory of Suicide Prevention/Crisis Agencies in the United States

(Courtesy American Association of Suicidology)

ALABAMA

Crisis Center of Jefferson County, Inc.
711 North Eighteenth Street
Birmingham, Ala. 35203

North Central Alabama Mental Health Center
304 Fourth Avenue S.E.
Decatur, Ala. 35601

Muscle Shoals Mental Health Center
(Suicide Prevention Center)
635 West College Street
Florence, Ala. 35630

ARIZONA

Mental Health Services
Suicide Prevention Center
1825 East Roosevelt
Phoenix, Ariz. 85006

Suicide and Crisis Center
801 South Prudence Road
Tucson, Ariz 85710

CALIFORNIA

Marilyn Adams Suicide Prevention Center of Bakersfield, Inc.
800 Eleventh Street
Bakersfield, California 93304

Note: A copy of the original directory, published by the American Association of Suicidology, which gives complete information about each of the centers, can be purchased, for the price of $5.00, from: Mrs. Charlotte Ross, Secretary, A. A. S., Suicide Prevention Center, 220 West Twentieth Avenue, San Mateo, California 94403.

CALIFORNIA (cont'd.)

Suicide Prevention of Santa Cruz County, Inc.
P. O. Box 36
Ben Lomond, Calif. 95005

Suicide Prevention of Almeda County, Inc.
P. O. Box 9102
Berkeley, Calif. 94709

Monterey County Suicide Prevention Center
P. O. Box 3241
Carmel, Calif. 93921

Help Line, Inc.
P. O. Box 5658
China Lake, Calif. 93555

Suicide Prevention of Davis
1620 North Anderson Road
Davis, Calif. 95616

Crisis House
630 West Lexington Avenue
El Cajon, Calif. 92020

Saddleback Valley "Help Line"
El Toro, Calif. 92630

North Bay Suicide Prevention, Inc.
1101 Union Avenue
Fairfield, Calif. 94533

Help in Emotional Trouble (H.E.T.)
1759 Fulton
Fresno, Calif. 93721

Hot Line—Garden Grove
Garden Grove Counseling Service
12345 Euclid Street
Garden Grove, Calif. 92640

New Hope 24 Hour Counseling Service
12141 Lewis Street
Garden Grove, Calif. 92640

"Help Now" Line
2750 Bellflower Boulevard
Long Beach, Calif. 90815

Help Line Contact Clinic
427 West Fifth Street
Los Angeles, Calif. 90013

Los Angeles Free Clinic
Psychological Counseling Department
115 North Fairfax
Los Angeles, Calif. 90036

Suicide Prevention Center and the Institute for Studies of Self-Destructive Behaviors
1041 South Menlo Avenue
Los Angeles, Calif. 90006

Suicide Prevention and Crisis Intervention Center
101 South Manchester Avenue
Orange, Calif. 92668

Suicide Crisis Intervention Center
Palm Springs Mental Health Clinic
1720 East Vista Chino
Palm Springs, Calif. 92262

Pasadena Mental Health Association
1815 North Fair Oaks
Pasadena, Calif. 19903

Psychiatric Crisis Clinic
Sacramento Medical Center
Emergency Area
2315 Stockton Boulevard
Sacramento, Calif. 95817

Suicide Prevention Service of Sacramento County, Inc.
P. O. Box 4463
Sacramento, Calif, 95825

Marin Suicide Prevention Center, Inc.
P. O. Box 792
San Anselmo, Calif, 94960

San Bernardino Suicide and Crisis Intervention Service
1999 North D Street
San Bernardino, California 92405

Community Crisis Center
3004 Imperial Avenue
San Diego, Calif. 92102

Center for Special Problems
2107 Van Ness Avenue
San Francisco, Calif, 94109

San Francisco Suicide Prevention, Inc.
307 Twelfth Avenue
San Francisco, California 94118

Suicide and Crisis Service
645 South Bascom Avenue
San Jose, Calif. 95128

Suicide Prevention Center of San Mateo County
220 West Twentieth Avenue
San Mateo, Calif. 94403

Marin Suicide Prevention Center, Inc.
P. O. Box 4212
San Rafael, Calif. 94947

Lifeline Crisis Servce, Inc.
P. O. Box 63
Stockton, Calif. 95201

North Bay Suicide Prevention
401 Amador Street
Vallejo, Calif. 94590

Ventura County Suicide Prevention Service
881 East Main Street
Ventura, Calif, 93001

Contra Costa Suicide Prevention
Teens and Twenties Crisis Intervention
P. O. Box 4852
Walnut Creek, Calif, 94596

COLORADO

Arapahoe Mental Health Center
Aurora Branch
551 Lansing
Aurora, Colo. 80010

COLORADO (cont'd.)
Suicidal Referral Service of El Paso County, Inc.
P. O. Box 1351
Colorado Springs, Colo. 80901

Emergency Psychiatric Service
Colorado General Hospital
4200 East Ninth Avenue
Denver, Colo. 80220

Emergency Room Psychiatric Services
Denver General Hospital
West Eighth Avenue and Bannock
Denver, Colo. 80206

Suicide and Crisis Control
2459 South Ash
Denver, Colo. 80222

Arapahoe Mental Health Center
4857 South Broadway
Englewood, Colo. 80110

Crisis Center and Suicide Prevention Center
499 Thirty Road
Grand Junction, Colo. 81501

Pueblo Suicide Prevention Service
1600 West Twenty-fourth Street
Pueblo, Colo. 81003

CONNECTICUT

Greater Bridgeport Community Mental Health Center
1862 East Main Street
Bridgeport, Conn. 06610

DELAWARE

Mental Health Emergency Service
863 South Governors Avenue
Dover, Del. 19901

Psychiatric Emergency Telephone Service
Sussex County Community Mental Health Center
Beebe Hospital of Sussex County, Inc.
Lewes, Del. 19958

Psychiatric Emergency Service
2001 North DuPont Parkway, Farnhurst
New Castle, Del. 19720

DISTRICT OF COLUMBIA

American University Multiple Emergency Center
Mary Graydon Center
Washington, D.C. 20002

Suicide Prevention and Emergency Mental Health Consultation Service
801 North Capitol Street, N.E.
Washington, D.C. 20002

FLORIDA

Suicide and Crisis Intervention Service, Inc.
804 S.W. Second Avenue
Gainesville, Fla. 32601

Suicide Prevention Center of
Jacksonville, Inc.
2627 Riverside Avenue
(P. O. Box 6393, 32205)
Jacksonville, Fla. 32205

Community Crisis Center, Inc.
125 S.W. Thirtieth Court
Miami, Fla. 33135

Personal Crisis Service
30 S.E. Eighth Street
Miami, Fla. 33131

We Care, Inc.
610 Mariposa
Orlando, Fla. 32801

Crisis and Suicide Intervention
Service
Brevard County Mental Health
Center, Inc.
1770 Cedar Street
Rockledge, Fla. 32955

Adult Mental Health Clinic
Pinellas County Emergency Service
vice
6170 Central Avenue
St. Petersburg, Fla. 33707

Crisis Line
707 Chillingworth Drive
West Palm Beach, Fla. 33401

GEORGIA

Fulton County Emergency Mental Health Service
tal Health Service
99 Butler Street, S.E.
Atlanta, Ga. 30303

HAWAII

Information and Referral Service
Suicide and Crisis Center
200 North Vineyard Boulevard
Honolulu, Hawaii 96817

ILLINOIS

St. Clair Counties Suicide Prevention Service, Inc.
tion Service, Inc.
200 North Illinois
Belleville, Ill.

Champaign County Suicide Prevention and Crisis Service
vention and Crisis Service
1206 South Randolph
Champaign, Ill. 61820

Crisis Intervention Program
4200 North Oak Park Avenue
Chicago, Ill. 60634

Illiana Institute of Drug and Emotional Problems
tional Problems
800 North Clark Street
Chicago, Ill. 60610

Crisis Counseling Service
Jefferson County Mental Health
Center
1300 Salem Road
Mount Vernon, Ill. 62864

Call For Help
320 East Armstrong Avenue
Peoria, Ill. 61603

ILLINOIS (cont'd.)
Suicide Prevention and Crisis
   Service
520 South Fourth Street
Quincy, Ill. 62301

Open Line Service
114 East Cherry Street
Watseka, Ill. 60970

INDIANA

Suicide Prevention Service
Marion County Association for
   Mental Health
1433 North Meridian Street
Indianapolis, Ind. 46202

IOWA

Lee County Mental Health Center
110 North Eighth Street
Keokuk, Iowa 52632

KANSAS

Area Mental Health Center
156 Gardendale
Garden City, Kans. 67846

Suicide Prevention Center
250 North 17
Kansas City, Kans. 66102

Can Help
P. O. Box 4253
Topeka, Kans. 66604

Suicide Prevention Service
1045 North Minneapolis
Wichita, Kans. 67214

LOUISIANA

The Phone
Student Health Service, LSU
Baton Rouge, La. 70803

MAINE

Dial Help
The Counseling Center
43 Illinois Avenue
Bangor, Maine 04401

Bath-Brunswick Area Rescue,
   Inc.
12 Whittier Street
Brunswick, Maine 04011

Rescue, Inc.
331 Cumberland Avenue
Portland, Maine 04101

MARYLAND

Crisis Intervention and Problem
   Solving Clinic of Sinai Hospital
   of Baltimore, Inc.
Bellvedere Avenue at Greenspring
Baltimore, Md. 21215

MASSACHUSETTS

Rescue, Inc.
115 Southampton Street
Boston, Mass. 02118

MICHIGAN

Call Someone Concerned
760 Riverside
Adrian, Mich.

Crisis Walk-In Center
208 North Fourth Avenue
Ann Arbor, Mich. 48108

Community Service Center (Chelsea)
775 South Main Street
Chelsea, Mich. 48118

Suicide Prevention Center
1151 Taylor Avenue
Detroit, Mich. 48202

Flint Regional Emergency Service
421 West Fifth Street
Flint, Mich. 48504

Suicide Prevention Crisis Intervention Service
Community Mental Health Clinic
Ottawa County Building
Grand Haven, Mich, 49417

Suicide Prevention and Crisis Intervention Service
Community Mental Health Clinic
549 West Eighteenth Street
Holland, Mich. 49423

Crisis Center
29200 Hoover Road
Warren, Mich. 48093

Ypsilanti Area Community Service
1637 Holmes Road
Ypsilanti, Mich. 48197

MINNESOTA

Crisis Intervention Center
Hennepin County General Hospital
Minneapolis, Minn. 55415

Emergency Social Service
413 Auditorium Street
St. Paul, Minn. 55102

Crisis, Inc.
744 Nineteenth Avenue, South
South St. Paul, Minn. 55075

MISSISSIPPI

Listening Post
P. O. Box 2072
Meridian, Miss. 39301

MISSOURI

Western Missouri Mental Health Center
Suicide Prevention Center
600 East Twenty-second Street
Kansas City, Mo. 64108

St. Joseph Suicide Prevention Service
Crisis Intervention
St. Joseph State Hospital
St. Joseph, Mo.

MISSOURI (cont'd.)
Suicide Prevention, Inc., of St.
 Louis
1118 Hampton Avenue
St. Louis, Mo. 63139

MONTANA

Blackfeet Crisis Center
Blackfeet Reservation
Browning, Mo. 59417

Great Falls Crisis Center
P. O. Box 124
Great Falls, Mo. 59403

NEBRASKA

Omaha Personal Crisis Service
P. O. Box 1491
Omaha, Nebr. 68101

NEVADA

Suicide Prevention and Crisis
 Call Center
Room 206 Mack SS Building
University of Nevada
Reno, Nev.

NEW HAMPSHIRE

North County Community Services, Inc.
227 Main Street
Berlin, N.H. 03570

NEW JERSEY

Ancora Suicide Prevention Ser-
 vice
Ancora Psychiatric Hospital
Hammonton, N.J. 08037

Middlesex County—Crisis Intervention
37 Oakwood Avenue
Metuchen, N.J. 08840

Crisis, Referral and Information
 (C.R.I.)
232 East Front Street
Plainfield, N.J. 07060

NEW MEXICO

The Crisis Center
Box 3563
University Park Br.
Las Cruces, New Mexico 88001

NEW YORK

Suicide Prevention Service
Kings County Hospital Center
606 Winthrop Street
Brooklyn, N.Y. 11203

Suicide Prevention and Crisis
 Service, Inc.
560 Main Street
Buffalo, N.Y. 14202

Lifeline
Nassau County Medical Center
2201 Hempstead Turnpike
East Meadow, N.Y. 11554

Suicide Prevention of Tompkins County, Inc.
P. O. Box 312
Ithaca, N.Y. 14850

Help Line Telephone Center
1 West Twenty-ninth Street
New York City, N.Y. 10001

National Save-A-Life League, Inc.
20 West Forty-third Street
New York City, N.Y. 10036

Niagara County Drug Hot Line and Crisis Intervention Service
910 Ferry Avenue
Niagara Falls, N.Y. 14303

24 Hour Mental Health Information and Crisis Phone Service
260 Crittenden Boulevard
Rochester, N.Y. 14620

Suicide Prevention Service
29 Sterling Avenue
White Plains, N.Y. 10606

NORTH CAROLINA

Durham County (N.C.) Mental Health Center
Crisis and Suicide Center
300 East Main Street
Durham, N.C. 27701

Crisis Help and Suicide Prevention Service of Gaston County
P. O. Box 3897
Akers Center Station
Gastonia, N.C. 28052

Crisis Control Center, Inc.
P. O. Box 735
Greensboro, N.C. 27402

Care
215 Mill Avenue
Jacksonville, N.C. 28542

Suicide and Crisis Intervention Service
Halifax County Mental Health Service
P. O. Box 577
Roanoke Rapids, N.C. 27870

Crisis and Suicide Intervention
P. O. Box Q
Sanford, N.C. 27330

NORTH DAKOTA

Suicide Prevention and Emergency Service
Ninth and Thayer
Bismarck, N.Dak. 58501

Suicide Prevention and Mental Health Center
700 First Avenue, South
Fargo, N.Dak. 58102

Northeast Regional Mental Health and Retardation Center
509 South Third Street
Grand Forks, N.Dak. 58201

St. Joseph's Hospital Suicide Prevention Center
St. Joseph's Hospital
Minot, N.Dak. 58701

OHIO

Support, Inc.
1361 West Market Street
Akron, Ohio 44313

Suicide Control Center
Mental Health Clinic of Ashtabula County
505 West Forty-sixth Street
Ashtabula, Ohio 44004

Crisis Intervention and Suicide Prevention
Athens Mental Health Center
Athens, Ohio 45701

The Suicide Prevention and Crisis Help Service of Stark County
2600 Sixth Street, S.W.
Canton, Ohio

Suicide Prevention
1515 East Broad Street
Columbus, Ohio 43205

Suicide Prevention Service
924 Harries Building
137 North Main Street
Dayton, Ohio 45402

Help Line Crisis Intervention Center
Counseling and Group Resources Center
Kent State University
Kent, Ohio 44240

Crisis Telephone Service, Inc.
114 Union Street
Newark, Ohio 43055

Rescue, Inc.
1933 Spielbusch Avenue
Toledo, Ohio 43624

Crisis Hotline
2845 Bell Street
Zanesville, Ohio 43701

OREGON

Crisis Service
127 N.A. Sixth Street
Corvallis, Oreg. 97330

Crisis Center
University of Oregon Counseling Center
Eugene, Oreg. 97403

PENNSYLVANIA

Lifeline
520 East Broad Street
Bethlehem, Pennsylvania 18018

Philadelphia Suicide Prevention Center
City Hall Annex, Room 430
Philadelphia, Pa. 19107

SOUTH CAROLINA

Crisis Intervention of Greenville
Greenville Area Mental Health Center
715 Grove Road
Greenville, S.C. 29605

TENNESSEE

Crisis Intervention Service
Helen Ross McNabb Center
1520 Cherokee Trail
Knoxville, Tenn. 37920

Suicide and Crisis Intervention
Service
P. O. Box 4068
Memphis, Tenn. 38104

Nashville Crisis Call Center
Meharry Community Mental
Health Center
Nashville, Tenn. 37209

TEXAS

Abilene Suicide Prevention Service
1333 North Second Street
P. O. Box 2707
Abilene, Tex. 79604

Suicide Prevention—Crisis Intervention
Box 3044
Amarillo, Tex. 79106

Suicide Prevention—Crisis Service
P. O. Box 3075
Corpus Christi, Tex. 78404

Suicide Prevention of Dallas, Inc.
P. O. Box 19651
Dallas, Tex. 75219

Crisis Intervention Service of the
Tarrant County Mental Health
and Mental Retardation Center
600 Texas Street
Fort Worth, Tex. 76102

San Antonio Suicide Prevention
Center
P. O. Box 10192
San Antonio, Tex. 78210

Concern
P. O. Box 1945
Wichita Falls, Tex. 76301

UTAH

Granite Community Mental Health
Center (Crisis Intervention
Service)
156 Westminster Avenue
Salt Lake City, Utah 84115

VIRGINIA

Suicide Crisis Center
Mayview Hospital
P. O. Box 6502
Portsmouth, Va. 23703

WASHINGTON

Crisis Clinic
3423 Sixth Street
Bremerton, Washington 98310

Emotional Crisis Service
1801 East Fourth
Olympia, Wash. 98501

WASHINGTON (cont'd.)
Crisis Clinic, Inc.
1701 Seventeenth Street
Seattle, Wash, 98122

Crisis Services
Community Mental Health Center
107 Division Street
Spokane, Wash. 99202

WEST VIRGINIA

Suicide Prevention Service
418 Morrison Building
815 Quarrier Street
Charleston, W.Va. 25301

Contact, Huntington
520 Eleventh Street
Huntington, W.Va. 25705

WISCONSIN

Suicide Prevention Center
310 Chestnut Street
Eau Claire, Wis. 54701

Walworth County Mental Health
   Center
P. O. Box 290
Elkhorn, Wis. 53121

Emergency Services
Dane County Mental Health Center
31 South Henry Street
Madison, Wis. 53703

Milwaukee County Mental Health
   Center
Psychiatric Emergency Services
8700 West Wisconsin Avenue
Milwaukee, Wis. 53226

WYOMING

Help Line, Inc.
Cheyenne, Wyo. 82001

CONTACT Teleministries U.S.A.

ALABAMA	South Baldwin County: Foley	205/943-5675
ARKANSAS	Hot Springs	501/623-2515
	Little Rock	501/666-0234
	Pine Bluff	501/536-4226
CALIFORNIA	Canoga Park	213/340-5433
	Garden Grove	714/639-4673
	Lafayette	415/284-2273
	Los Angeles	213/620-0144
	Pasadena	213/449-4500
	San Jose	408/287-9211
ILLINOIS	Lake County: Waukegan	312/336-6416
	Rockford	815/964-4044
INDIANA	Anderson	317/649-5211
	Gary/Merrillville	219/769-3141
	New Albany/Jeffersonville	812/945-1167
MINNESOTA	Minneapolis/St. Paul	612/341-2896
MISSISSIPPI	Jackson	601/362-2525
MISSOURI	St. Charles	314/Enterprise 41143
	St. Louis	314/725-3022
NEW HAMPSHIRE	Derry	603/434-4511
NEW JERSEY	Atlantic County: Pleasantville	609/646-6616
	Burlington County: Willingboro	609/871-4700
	Moorestown	609/461-4700
	Mt. Holly	609/267-8500
	Cherry Hill	609/667-3000
	Elizabeth	201/527-0555
	Hudson County: Jersey City	201/451-9100
NEW YORK	New York City	212/686-3061
	Syracuse	315/445-1500
NORTH CAROLINA	Charlotte	704/333-6121
	Durham	919/683-1595

Note: Reprinted by permission of Contact Teleministries U.S.A., Inc., 900 S. Arlington Avenue, Harrisburg, Pennsylvania 17109.

NORTH CAROLINA (cont'd.)

	Fayetteville	919/485-4134
	High Point	919/882-8121
	Johnson County: Smithfield	919/934-6161
	Rocky Mount	919/443-5144
	Winston-Salem	919/722-5153
OHIO	Ashtabula County: Ashtabula	216/998-2607
	Cincinnati	513/631-0111
	Trumbull County: Warren	216/393-1565
	Niles	216/544-2707
	Cortland	216/637-9516
OKLAHOMA	Enid	405/234-1111
	Oklahoma City	405/236-0551
	Perry	405/Enterprise 53620
PENNSYLVANIA	Chambersburg	717/264-7799
	Harrisburg	717/652-4400
	Philadelphia	215/879-4402
	Pittsburgh	412/782-4024
	York	717/845-3656
SOUTH CAROLINA	Columbia	803/782-9222
	Rock Hill	803/328-8205
TENNESSEE	Chattanooga	615/622-5193
	Cleveland	615/479-9666
	McMinn/Meigs Counties: Athens	615/745-9111
	Oak Ridge, TN	615/482-4949
TEXAS	Arlington/Mid-Cities	817/277-2233
	Dallas	214/522-7788
	Lubbock	806/765-8393
VIRGINIA	Martinsville/Henry County	703/632-7295
	Newport News	804/245-0041
	Virginia Beach	804/428-2211
WEST VIRGINIA	Charleston	304/346-0826
	Huntington	304/523-3448
WISCONSIN	Milwaukee	414/342-5669

LIFE LINE International
210 Pitt Street
Sydney, N.S.W. 2000
Australia

Notes

CHAPTER 2

1. Ben Haden, *Rebel to Rebel* (Miami: Logoi, 1971).

CHAPTER 3

1. Earl A. Grollman, *Suicide* (Boston: Beacon Press, 1971).

CHAPTER 5

1. Quoted in Elisabeth Elliot, *Shadow of the Almighty* (Grand Rapids, Mich.: Zondervan, 1970).
2. Duane Pederson, *On Lonely Street with God* (New York: Hawthorn Books, 1973).
3. J. Wallace Hamilton, *What About Tomorrow?* (Old Tappan, N.J.: Fleming H. Revell Co., 1972).

CHAPTER 6

1. J. Wallace Hamilton, *What About Tomorrow?* (Old Tappan, N.J.: Fleming H. Revell Co., 1972).
2. Kenneth L. Wilson, *Have Faith Without Fear* (New York: Harper and Row, 1970).
3. Paul W. Pretzel, *Understanding and Counseling the Suicidal Person* (Nashville, Tenn.: Abingdon Press, 1972).
4. Wilson, *Have Faith Without Fear*.
5. Hamilton, *What About Tomorrow?*
6. Ibid., p. 59.
7. Ibid., pp. 63–64.
8. Ibid., p. 65.

CHAPTER 7

1. Harry A. Ironside, *Acts* (Neptune, N.J.: Loizeaux), p. 381.
2. Ibid.
3. A. Alvarez, *The Savage God* (New York: Random House, 1972).
4. Ibid.
5. Ibid.

CHAPTER 8

1. A. Alvarez, *The Savage God* (New York: Random House, 1972).
2. Earl A. Grollman, *Suicide* (Boston: Beacon Press, 1971).
3. Ibid.
4. Alvarez, *The Savage God*.
5. Paul W. Pretzel, *Understanding and Counseling the Suicidal Person* (Nashville, Tenn.: Abingdon Press, 1972).
6. Alvarez, *The Savage God*.
7. Ibid.
8. Ibid.

CHAPTER 9

1. E. S. Schneidman, *Essays in Self-Destruction* (New York: International Science Press, 1967).
2. Earl A. Grollman, *Suicide* (Boston: Beacon Press, 1971).
3. "Up from Suicide" (editorial), *Christianity Today,* June 9, 1972.
4. Grollman, *Suicide*.

CHAPTER 10

1. Sigmund Freud, *Civilization and Its Discontents* (New York: Norton, 1962); and "Morning and Melancholia," *Collected Papers,* Volume II (London: The Hogarth Press, 1949).
2. Karl A. Menninger, *Man Against Himself* (New York: Harcourt, Brace, 1938).
3. Russell Palmer, *The Lengthening Shadow of Suicide* (Chicago: Claretian Publications, 1965).
4. Menninger, *Man Against Himself*.

CHAPTER 11

1. Maurice L. Farber, *Theory of Suicide* (New York: Funk and Wagnalls, 1968).
2. "Go to the Top for Help," *These Times,* November 1972.
3. A. Alvarez, *The Savage God* (New York: Random House, 1972).
4. Sylvia Plath, *The Bell Jar* (New York: Harper and Row, 1971).
5. Ibid.
6. Alvarez, *The Savage God*.
7. Eliot Asinof, *Craig and Joan: Two Lives for Peace* (New York: Viking Press, 1971).
8. Quoted in J. B. Phillips (ed.), *The New Testament in Modern English* (New York: Macmillan, 1972).